Francisco -

One year ago today you told me that you loved me for the first time. I'm looking forward to sharing a lifetime of that love.

Always,

Ann

February 23, 1999

PRAISE FOR *How We Met*

"Engaging, charming, and altogether romantic."
—JONATHAN KELLERMAN, bestselling author

⁓

"This book displays solid execution of a fascinating idea
and provides an abundance of engaging,
touching true stories."
—MICHAEL MEDVED, film critic and author of *Saving Childhood*

⁓

"I thought this would be a fluff book on love stories.
Instead, it was a banquet that fed my heart and soul.
This book is for anyone who believes that true love
does exist. Here are powerful, memorable
stories to savor and relish."
—KRYSTA KAVENAUGH, managing editor, *Marriage* magazine

How We Met

Chance Encounters
and Other True
Love Stories of
Real-Life Couples

Miriam Sokol

PRIMA PUBLISHING

PRIMA PUBLISHING and colophon are registered trademarks of Prima Communications, Inc.

Library of Congress Cataloging-in-Publication Data

Sokol, Miriam.
How we met: chance encounters and other true love stories of
real-life couples, Miriam Sokol.
p. cm.
ISBN 0-7615-1704-9
1. Love. 2. Man–woman relationships. 3. Dating (Social customs). I. Title.
HQ801.A3S67 1998
306.7—dc21 98-50843
CIP

99 00 01 02 03 HH 10 9 8 7 6 5 4 3 2 1
Printed in the United States of America

Interior design by Trina Stahl and Dover Publications

HOW TO ORDER
Single copies may be ordered from Prima Publishing, P.O. Box 1260BK, Rocklin, CA 95677; telephone (916) 632-4400. Quantity discounts are also available. On your letterhead, include information concerning the intended use of the books and the number of books you wish to purchase.

Visit us online at www.primalife.com

To my husband, Stacy,
for all the diamonds we have polished.

Contents

◜‿◝

CONTENTS

CONTENTS

Acknowledgments

I WANT TO thank all the couples who openly shared some of their most precious and intimate moments and permitted their stories to be told. Your accounts will bring hope to single people still in search of a partner, and will undoubtedly recall in married couples loving memories of their own first moments together. In our discussions about how you met your partners, without my prodding, many of you referred to your spouses as your soul mates. After hearing your tales, a mix of triumph, sometimes pain, and always love, I believe you were indeed blessed with finding your "soul mate."

I thank my good friends—Shoshana Brickman, Marla Schechter, Marcia Golan, and Beth Shmagin, and especially my mom, Esther, and my two sisters, Naomi Berkowitz and Sigi Siegel, for reading early drafts of my stories and for your comments and incisive analysis. Mark Ellman, your enthusiasm and encouragement at the very beginning was the fuel that kept me going. Thank you, Shoshana, for always being on the lookout for a good story.

I want to acknowledge my teachers in Jerusalem and in Los Angeles, who, by your erudite and intelligent instruction, literally opened new worlds to me. Through your teachings, you communicated a more noble reality infused with holiness and rich with the infinite potential of the human spirit. In some small way, I hope, by this book, to have passed on the word.

Torah derivative texts provided the sources for the expository sections of this book. There is much to learn about the workings of the soul and the concept of soul mates that is beyond the scope of this book. I want to thank the Science of Kabbalah Institute in Chicago for teaching and clarifying complex mystical ideas about the soul and soul mates in a clear and exciting manner.

I want to thank my agent, Jeff Herman, for taking me on board.

Thanks to my editors, Michelle McCormack and Denise Sternad, for your continuous energy and enthusiasm and valuable insights.

I cannot thank my husband enough for his unwaivering support; for crying "on cue" at the end of many of the stories (the test, I found, for a good story); for taking the kids out on Sundays; and among his many abilities, for proving to be an incredibly skillful editor and my best friend.

With gratitude to the One whose hand is in every match, just below the surface.

A Roman matron once asked a sage, "Now that God has finished creating the universe, what does He do?"
The sage replied, "He is busy making matches."

Introduction

MARRIED COUPLES ARE often asked, "How did you two meet?" Often, the husband and wife will look at each other, break into smiles, and then, with remarkable detail, tell their own unique and sometimes amazing story.

Couples meet in countless ways: Some do so early in life and never look back; some search for years, seemingly moving heaven and earth to find a match; and some meet by accident, thrown together by chance repeatedly until one day there's a spark and romance blossoms. All of the true-life accounts in this book are testaments to this underlying, universal story: the unique journey of two souls to find each other and forge an inexplicably powerful bond.

Is it fate or destiny that brings two people together? Many of the couples in this book believe they were destined to meet, and the idea that two people are "made for each other" goes back a long way. One ancient parable says that forty days before conception a heavenly voice calls out and proclaims, "This daughter will be for that son." When two people manage to meet, fall in love, and create a life together despite the myriad obstacles in their way—especially in our modern world—it's hard not to believe that something of the divine isn't guiding them together.

The paradigm for the parable, of course, is the story of Adam and Eve. In the book of Genesis, God created Adam as one androgynous being with a complete soul of his own. Then he split Adam in half, creating man and woman, who each possessed half a soul. Only when joined together could they recreate their original wholeness. Adam and Eve, the progenitors of humankind, were the original soul mates—the first blueprint.

Plato also advanced the idea of a soul mate. "Platonic love" is not asexual love, as it is commonly understood, but rather the spiritual attraction of one soul to its original mate. Plato considered it the highest form of human love.

Some mystics also describe a "treasury of souls" where souls harmoniously contain both masculine and feminine properties. When a soul decides to inhabit a body—which is the only way it can accomplish its destiny—it must split in two and become a man or a woman. These mystics believe that, although our soul's purpose is never completely revealed to us, one of the soul's driving forces is to connect with its other half. The concept of the soul mate is the stuff of romantic novels, but it is also at the root of many religious and spiritual beliefs.

THEN AGAIN, Adam and Eve weren't exactly faced with a wide array of choices. How can we know if we have met our soul mate? Are there any clues? Some people say, "I just know." Sometimes a couple's chemistry is unmistakable—an intangible connection that transcends physical attraction, almost like a sixth sense. But for many of us, despite the intensity of our romantic feelings, such a clear sense of destiny or fate is missing, and in fact, we can never be completely certain. But we can learn to listen closer to our instincts and to trust our inner sense.

At first glance, our lives may appear to be a series of unrelated events, without purpose, without direction. But if we look back and dissect the pieces of the puzzle, we see that the events that brought us to the present day are more significant than they seemed. What if I never missed that flight, which I was so upset about at the time? What if a friend had not spent thirty minutes convincing me to go to that party until, reluctantly, I caved in? Who would have dreamed that dialing a wrong number would lead to matrimony? Individually, these are just tiny details, holding nothing like the weight of destiny. But linked together, they form the quiet miracles that shape and direct our lives, and which we can come to recognize if we pay attention.

Most people believe that if two people are destined to meet, they will meet—even if it takes a miracle—and the stories in this book bear this out. Many of these couples have indeed met through amazing circumstances. In particular, it is astonishing how many couples have known each other before, or have actually been together as a couple, but who become separated only to reunite years later. These stories prove that if we miss each other the first time—if we are too young or not ready, or if something else keeps us apart—it is as if heaven sends its angels to guide us back together, giving us a second chance. Even the most seemingly ordinary meetings—although, I believe, there are no ordinary meetings—reveal a divine plan.

This book is a collection of true stories about how couples

met despite great odds and unusual circumstances. These are real people, and their humanity—their kindness and courage, their weakness and failings—comes through most clearly. We see their struggles, their doubts and uncertainties, and we see their triumphs as well; they are our mirrors.

Most of the stories in this book end when the couple ties the knot, and it is tempting to add on the end of each one: ". . . and they lived happily ever after." But there is a larger story these couples continue to live, that of marriage itself. Finding your soul mate does not make marriage any less difficult. New challenges present themselves, and we must learn to give and to compromise, to control our baser instincts, and to do things and take on tasks we don't especially like or want to do. From a spiritual perspective, this is part of the work our souls are here to do, and learning to control our destructive drives and to give when we find it difficult is a supreme accomplishment.

We all hope, one day, to meet that special person, the one who seems made just for us. If we've been in a lot of relationships and have yet to find the one where our heart says yes, we may begin to despair, feeling we are doomed to be alone. If that describes you, take heart. Destiny may be right next to you and you don't yet see it. If nothing else, the stories gathered here are all vivid reminders of the strange and unexpected pathways of the soul.

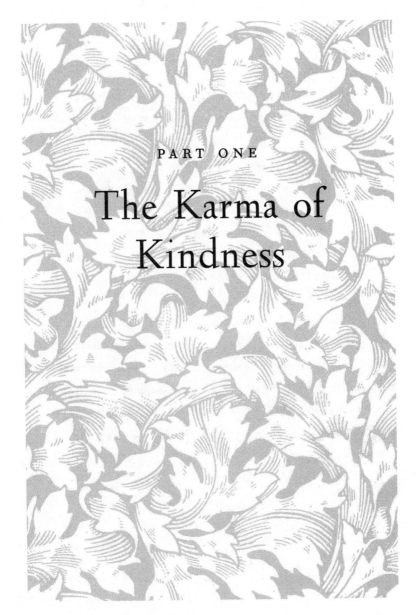

PART ONE

The Karma of Kindness

MANY of us have heard of the concept of karma. Even if you've never heard the word, you're most likely familiar with the concept "what goes around comes around" and that there are indeed consequences to all actions, both good and bad. According to spiritual teachings, our actions transcend the physical world and reach into the spiritual world, creating positive or negative energy. These energies transform into powerful spiritual forces—some call them angels—that in turn influence the physical world.

For most of us, the idea of spiritual reality is hard to grasp. And for the most part, we are not directly aware of the consequences of things we do and say and even think. But sometimes we do see a karmic balance at work. In these stories, acts of kindness seem to be rewarded—by the meeting and recognition of people who are meant to be together.

Through the Barbed Wire

~

IN 1941, DURING World War II, Herman and his mother were living in the Jewish ghetto of Pioktow in Poland—where they had been forced to move two years earlier—when German soldiers rounded them up with other ghetto inhabitants to be taken to Treblinka, one of the Nazi-run death camps. Herman was twelve years old, and he clung fiercely to his mother while they waited to be boarded onto cattle cars. His mother, who understood what was happening, pushed him away, scolding her son: "You're no longer a child. Leave me. Get away!" Herman protested, but his mother continued to shout at him until, confused and scared, he finally ran off. It was the last time he would see her.

During the next year and a half, Herman was transferred from the ghetto to two concentration camps and then, eventually, to Schleiben, a work camp seventy miles outside of Berlin. There, he slept in filthy, crowded barracks with other men and teenage boys, who were worked until they collapsed, whether from exhaustion, disease, or the constant blows of the guards. But still, the worst was hunger. Each worker was given

3

a daily ration of one slice of bread and some watery soup, and nothing more. Herman watched as men slowly starved to death. Every morning, those who didn't survive the night were carted away.

One bitter and cold winter day in February 1944, Herman stood shivering near the barbed wire that enclosed the perimeter of the camp, which adjoined a farm. His tattered prison clothes hung loosely about him, and his feet were wrapped in rags. He noticed a little girl standing outside, staring at him. When she saw that Herman had seen her, she approached.

Consumed with hunger, Herman looked around to make sure no guards were nearby, and then he asked in German, "Can you bring me something to eat?"

"I don't understand German," the girl responded.

Herman asked again in Polish. For a moment, she just looked at him with her brown, round eyes, and then she nodded—she would come tomorrow—and scurried away.

The next day at the same time, the little girl appeared by the barbed-wire fence. When Herman saw that no one was looking, he dashed over while she quickly tossed him a scrap of bread and an apple. He grabbed the food, hid it in his pocket, and ran back to the camp, where, in secret, he cut the bread into tiny pieces so he could eat little bits throughout the day.

If caught, Herman knew his punishment would be death. He could barely hope the little girl would come again, but the next day she was waiting at the same spot, her hands buried beneath her coat, concealing food she had brought.

Instinctively, the eight-year-old girl never told her parents about her new friend; they would have forbidden any further meetings. Every day for seven months she waited for him at the usual time, tossing over bits of food when he approached and then hurrying away. When extra food was hard to come by, she parceled out her own. They never spoke or exchanged names.

One day, Herman approached the fence more slowly than usual, calling out, "Girl!"

She came close.

"Don't come around anymore," he warned. "I am being transferred to Theresiensdadt." She looked at him inquisitively.

"It's in Czechoslovakia," he explained. "I'm leaving tomorrow."

Her eyes widened and filled with tears. She knew she would never see him again. Herman held his head low as he walked away, trying to hold back his own tears. But his chest heaved with sadness and fear, and when he turned around to look at her, he couldn't contain himself anymore.

By 1945, the last year of the war, the notorious gas chamber had arrived in Theresiensdadt, and it was used at an increasingly frenzied pace to kill the camp's inmates as Allied Forces pushed across Europe and closed in. Before dawn on May 8, 1945, Herman woke to the wild shouting of a Nazi SS guard: He informed the enfeebled inmates that they would all be going to "the showers"—in other words, death in the gas chambers—at ten o'clock that morning. But at 8 A.M., Herman and the rest of the concentration camp survivors were saved when Allied Forces liberated the camp.

After the war, Herman went to Israel, where he recovered his strength and began to rebuild his life. He became a soldier and fought in Israel's 1948 War of Independence. But after a few years, he grew tired of war and fighting, and in 1950 he left for good to New York City.

HERMAN WAS tall and broad-shouldered, articulate and mature beyond his years. He had street smarts, but was prone to pensiveness on occasion. This was, he found, a combination that was irresistible to women, and he began to date seriously for the first time in his life. In fact, over the next few years, Herman was engaged to be married three separate times. But each time, an instinct drove him to break off the matches, despite the disappointment and sadness of the forsaken women.

Having developed a dismal engagement history, Herman decided not to become seriously involved with anyone for a while, though his friends continued to fix him up now and again with blind dates. One day several years later, a friend insisted he meet Roma, a woman with dark hair and lively brown eyes.

Herman agreed, and his friend arranged a double date. Herman found Roma to be beautiful, outspoken, and kind. Although she radiated gentleness, she was also strong, with a firm belief in herself and her ideas. They talked all night and never ran out of things to say. They learned, to their surprise, that Roma had been a nurse in Israel when Herman had been a soldier. They had even been at the same social events, but they had never met. Herman found himself unexpectedly falling in love with the young woman.

At the end of the evening, Herman and Roma were in the backseat as Herman's friend drove Roma home. Their conversation turned to the war.

"I was in a work camp most of the war outside Berlin. Schleiben," Herman told her.

"I know where Schleiben is," she said, struck by the coincidence. "I was also in Schleiben. My family, we were disguised as Christian farmers working in the fields near the camp. A priest had helped us with false identification papers. He saved our lives." Herman listened with growing interest as she continued. "I wasn't in the camp, of course. But I met a boy there. He was starving. He asked me for food. So I brought food for a while. I would toss it over the fence."

"What did the boy look like?" Herman asked.

"Well," she said, pausing to recall. "He was about thirteen or fourteen. Very, very thin. I was just a girl, but I could see he was starving "

"What did he eat?"

"Bread mostly. Sometimes I could also get some apples," she replied.

"How long did you meet him there?" Herman, now sitting upright, had inched his way to the edge of the seat.

"Seven months," she answered. Herman's heart was pounding.

He asked her a few more questions, and when each answer matched his knowledge of those events, he began to tremble.

Herman asked quietly, his voice faltering, "Did he tell you he was being transferred to Theresiensdadt and not to come around anymore?"

"Yes," she said. "That's exactly what he said." She looked at him strangely. How could he possibly know that?

Herman fell against the back of his seat, stunned. Sitting beside him was the Polish farm girl who had saved his life.

"I was that boy," Herman whispered, more to himself than to her.

"How can this be?" Roma asked. She couldn't believe that

Herman could be the boy from the camp—it was impossible. "Tell me," she asked, almost hesitating, "did you wear rags for shoes on your feet?" He nodded.

Roma's eyes moistened with tears as she took in the amazing truth, and they embraced for the first time.

Herman proposed to Roma before the car reached her apartment. The two were married in New York City in 1959. Today, they have two children and several grandchildren. Herman believes fate saved him from death several times in the concentration camps—and, not to mention, from three marriages to other women—so that he could reunite with his soul mate fifteen years after their harrowing childhood meeting.

Kindred Spirits

⌐◠⌐

$\mathcal{A}$s TESS PREPARED to go to a friend's dinner party one evening, she sat in front of a mirror examining her face: Her high, regal cheekbones and pale skin were still framed by pretty, reddish hair, but there was no denying that she looked older. Where had all the years gone? she wondered. She scanned her past, trying to account for the years like misplaced objects. She had always assumed that by now she would be married, with children, and here she was still single. She sighed. Why hadn't she married as she'd wanted to, as everyone believed she would? Had she let the right person go by? Had she failed to seize an opportunity? Was it her fault, the fault of the men she'd dated, or was there just no one meant for her? In the end, she'd found no definitive answers, and she had to reach a difficult conclusion: Maybe she would never marry.

Once she'd learned to accept this possibility, she felt strangely free. She was a successful professional, with a quick, perceptive mind, and she began to focus on the things that gave her pleasure and satisfaction. She was naturally happy and optimistic, and she continued to cultivate her circle of friends and

9

to meet the challenges of her work. After a while, when well-meaning friends tried to set her up on blind dates, she simply refused.

"Tess, you can't be so picky," they told her. "You're not getting any younger."

Comments like that always caused her a twinge of regret, but she had learned it did no good to dwell on the things she couldn't change, and as she finished preparing for her friend's party, she was thankful to feel she had moved on with her life.

At dinner, she sat across from a man named Steven, who sat in a wheelchair. He didn't have the use of his arms or legs, and he breathed with the aid of a ventilator. They spoke periodically throughout the evening, and Tess was struck by how handsome he was. He had the large frame of an athlete and a face that could grace the cover of a male fashion magazine. He smiled readily and was an eager participant in the lively conversations that darted around the table. What a large spirit he seems to have, Tess thought, as if he were untouched by tragedy. Through his atrophied muscles, she saw a hidden grace.

Tess got Steven's telephone number from her friend and called him a few days later. She was intrigued by this young man, and she asked if she could come visit sometime. Steven quickly agreed and welcomed her any time.

The first day Tess decided to visit, Steven's caretaker, Mark, opened the front door and quickly disappeared into another room. As Tess entered the small, sparsely furnished apartment, Steven looked up and threw her a wide smile.

"What a great surprise!" he said. "Come in. Sit down." He looked to the room where the caretaker had vanished. "Would you like something to drink?"

"Oh, I'm fine. I just came to chat." They fell into easy conversation, mostly about Tess. Steven didn't focus on himself very much; he made jokes and flattered her, taking an intense interest in everything she had to say.

Tess continued to visit Steven, and gradually she learned more about his history: He had graduated summa cum laude at his university, where he had also been an athlete of some renown. In his early twenties, he began having some unusual nerve quivers, and he was diagnosed with Lou Gehrig's disease. Now, at age thirty, he was confined entirely to his wheelchair, and his physical care was completely in the hands of others. He had adapted, however; his mind was as sharp and active as ever.

One summer morning, Tess rose early. I think I'll surprise Steven with a visit in the afternoon, she thought. They lived in Cape Town, South Africa, and it was an exceptionally hot day—humid and stale, lacking the usual breezes that blew gently across the city.

Tess was panting by the time she reached Steven's apartment, and as she knocked, the door fell open. She entered cautiously. Before she could call out his name, Tess saw Steven sitting near an unopened window, streaks of sweat dripping down his face and neck, drenching his clothes. The apartment was unbearably hot. How had this happened? Tess darted to each window and opened them, shaking with anger. Finally, she faced Steven and tried to compose herself. He sat limp, unsmiling.

"Where is Mark?" she asked sharply.

"He went out."

"How long have you been here alone?"

"A few hours."

"A few hours!" she cried. "In this heat? And the windows closed shut! Oh, how thoughtless!"

Tess got Steven a glass of ice water and helped him drink it. She bathed his forehead and neck with a cold, wet washcloth to cool him down. Then she grabbed the handles of his wheelchair and headed for the door.

"We're going for a walk. Let's get something to eat in an air-conditioned restaurant."

After that incident, Tess took an even greater and more personal interest in Steven's well-being. She visited him often, sometimes bringing friends to spend the evenings with them. She learned to disassemble his wheelchair and help him get in and out of her car.

Together they explored Cape Town. One of their favorite places was a park filled with colorful gardens and trees in the full bloom of summer. They would stroll among the exotic plants for hours and then picnic on the grounds with the sweet fragrance of jasmine all around.

One day, Steven's caretaker suddenly gave notice that he was quitting, and Tess insisted on helping Steven find a new one. It would be no small task. The first one they hired they fired after three days when they caught him stealing Steven's money.

While they hired a temp to look after Steven, Tess doubled her efforts. She placed ads in the papers and scrawled "Help Wanted" on index cards and posted them in all the neighborhood restaurants. She interviewed all the applicants who responded—a motley collection of petty criminals, down-and-outs, and virtual illiterates—and promptly rejected each one. She called her friends and associates for referrals until—finally—she received a solid recommendation for an experienced male nurse. When she got a phone call from another applicant the next day, she was not very interested in talking to him; she felt certain the referral would work out.

"Oh yes," she said distractedly. "The position's still open, but . . ." Her voice trailed off.

On the other end of the line, Jerry waited for her to complete her sentence. He had arrived from New York that same week, at two o'clock in the morning, crossing the ocean to South Africa and hoping to create a different life for himself. Later that first morning, he had gone to a diner, ordered coffee, and then scanned the newspaper's classified ads for hours. Nothing called out to him. Finally, his body sore from sitting so long, he got up to go, and as he walked out of the restaurant, his eye caught one of Tess's "Help Wanted" index cards. He immediately phoned the number.

The silence stretched on.

"Hello?" Jerry said.

"Oh, I'm sorry," Tess replied, becoming professional again. "Do you have any references?"

"I can give you some business references—"

"You don't have experience in this kind of work?" she interrupted, impatient. Why did everyone, experienced or not, think they could do this job? She ended the call immediately, saying, "Well, we are interviewing a few prospects. Please call back in a few days."

When Tess briefly mentioned the call to Steven later, he chided her gently.

"Tess," he said, "I've been at this longer than you. We have to consider everyone. The referral may not work out."

"I know, I know," she agreed. But in her heart she knew the referral was the one.

"Not everything is in our hands," Steven said, his eyes glancing heavenward.

As it ended up, the referral did not work out. So when Jerry called again in a few days to ask if the position was still open, Tess agreed to meet him that afternoon.

When Jerry arrived at the door of Steven's apartment, Tess sized him up right away: medium height; powerfully built; dark hair; calm, soft eyes; and a pleasant manner. Her previous naïveté had left her cautious, and she became severe and professional as she interviewed him.

"So," she asked him sharply, "you've only been in Cape Town for a few days?"

"Yes. I'm staying with some friends."

"And you say you have no experience in this kind of work?"

"No, I don't, but I'm a quick learner. One of my jobs in New York was hauling boxes."

"I see," Tess said, unimpressed. "But this job needs more than just strong arms."

"I've been known to be pretty decent at chess," Jerry said lightly, smiling.

Steven silently watched the exchange, and for him the decision was easy: He liked Jerry immediately. "When can you start?" he asked, interrupting them.

Tess looked at Steven, wincing. "But Steven—"

"It's all right, Tess. I have an instinct for this."

She could see by the look in his eye that the matter was settled.

"Are you two family?" Jerry asked Tess.

"No," Tess answered, softening a little and smiling. "No, we're just friends." As she said it, she realized just how much she cared for Steven and how protective she had become. He *had* become part of her family, and for a brief moment, Jerry saw a different woman as all these emotions played across Tess's face.

Jerry became the caretaker they had dreamed of. As promised, he was a quick learner and extremely capable. But his true gift was his easy, pleasant manner and the way he accepted his destiny in matters small and large. It was his particular charm to find joy in all he did, and he soon became Steven's friend.

As the weeks passed, Jerry joined Steven, Tess, and their various other friends on their forays around the city. At a moment's notice, Tess would pack a full picnic and drag everyone along to the beach or the park, transforming everything they did into an adventure. At these outings, Jerry would find ways to be near Tess when they were a little apart from the rest of the group and engage her in private conversation.

Several months after Jerry's arrival, Steven took a long trip to visit relatives in another city. During Steven's absence, Jerry found excuses to meet up with Tess, and although she appreciated Jerry's attention and friendship, she did not think much more of it than that. After all, he was younger than she. He could never be interested in me in *that* way, Tess thought, even though, when she allowed herself to admit it, she found herself attracted to him and now secretly looked forward to their times alone together.

Then, one balmy evening they met for dinner, and afterward they took a walk near the beach. They talked quietly, easily, sometimes letting the conversation drift into silence, simply listening to the sound of the water and the pleasant tap of Tess's sandals on the pavement. Every now and then, Jerry turned to look at Tess, trying to summon the words. After a while, he stopped, turned to face her, and took her hands.

"Marry me," he said softly.

Tess was taken by complete surprise. She could hardly believe he meant it.

"Jerry," Tess protested mildly, "you don't know how old I am."

"I don't care. I know you're older than I am. But it feels right to be with you. I can't imagine one day without you. I want you to marry me," he said again, more insistent this time.

Tess started to cry, and then she nodded her head. Yes, of course—her heart bursting with long-withheld sorrow and unexpected joy—she would marry him.

WHEN HE returned home, Steven was delighted to hear the news. He had seen immediately what Tess hadn't—she and Jerry were kindred spirits all along.

Tess and Jerry married several months later in a simple but joyous ceremony. Guests at the wedding said they had never felt the presence of so much love and goodwill. For Tess, it seemed like all her years of waiting and then of letting go of her desire to be married had been necessary for her to find Jerry. Though Jerry is no longer Steven's caretaker, the three friends still get together often.

PART TWO

Dream, Dream, Dream

WHAT *are dreams? And what does it mean when we encounter dream images in waking life? Some say that when we sleep, portions of our souls actually interact with other souls in the spiritual world, and we receive messages from this world through our dreams. Certain mystics claim the feeling of falling we so often experience while dreaming is actually the descent of our souls back into our bodies.*

Dreams are an evocative enigma, and certainly some are no more than a product of a spicy meal, a stressful event, or hormonal influences. There are times, however, when dreams contain startlingly clear images and voices that either foretell the future or guide us in some important decision. Sometimes an obscure but powerful dream image will stay with us for days until something happens that reveals its message. These are undoubtedly communications from the soul world, and every now and then, one is the link that brings two people together.

A Skeptic Believes

$\mathcal{P}$HILIP, THE SON of an Italian father and French mother, grew up in Sweden. Though his parents were both Catholics, they raised him with little religious feeling or spiritual beliefs. Instead, they encouraged him to develop his physical talents, and as a young man, he became highly skilled at judo. He became a member of the Swedish national judo team and traveled with the squad all over Europe, developing a taste for food, wine, and art. Eventually, at age twenty-nine, a model he'd been dating in Paris convinced him to move with her to Southern California.

Though the relationship ended, Philip stayed in California, and his natural athleticism led to a career as a weight trainer. He enjoyed nothing more than the feel of cool steel in his hands and the warm rush of adrenaline after an intense workout. He was at ease in the physical world and would scoff at spiritual things, believing there was nothing more to reality than what he could see and touch. Attractive and friendly, Philip had no trouble dating, but his relationships never moved past the dating stage. He never minded. He was perfectly comfortable with the life he'd created . . . until one night when a mysterious dream changed everything.

In the dream, a woman's face appeared in remarkable detail. She was petite and slightly older than Philip, with black hair, brown eyes, and a radiant smile. An unfamiliar voice, low and gentle, said, "This is the woman you should spend the rest of your life with." Still dreaming, Philip tried to dismiss the imagery.

But the voice repeated itself: "This is the woman you should spend the rest of your life with."

Again Philip tried to banish the image, but the face remained and the voice repeated the message for a third time.

Then, just as suddenly, the dream ended.

Philip awoke the next morning unnerved. For the rest of the day, the dream stayed with him, remaining extremely vivid and clear. As much as he tried to drive it out of his head, he could not. This is insane, he thought.

Who was that woman? All day he wracked his brain, but he couldn't place her. He thought she must be a stranger. But later, as the dream replayed itself again and again, he remembered: He had met her several years ago at a dinner party thrown by a friend. He had talked to almost everyone there, but he had never had a chance to meet her—or her husband.

Husband! She was married! This is nuts, he thought to himself, and he immediately resolved to forget the whole thing. He would keep the experience to himself, and in a few days, he believed, he would forget it ever happened.

The next night he went to a party that he'd been invited to several weeks earlier. He was having a good time, chatting with other guests and helping the host serve drinks. He'd only been there a half an hour when a woman walked in. Glancing up, Philip could hardly believe his eyes: She was the woman in his dream.

She looked exactly the same: petite, with brown eyes and black hair—very pretty, and several years older than him. And she was alone. Though Philip didn't know it yet, she had divorced two years earlier.

Their eyes met and locked, and they both felt an inexplicable connection. She walked toward him, their eyes never wavering. Entranced, Philip asked her if she wanted a drink. Normally, he disdained notions like love at first sight, but no other words could explain what he was feeling right then—this intense, immediate, powerful tug to be near her, to know her. Later, she would tell him she felt the same thing, something she had never felt with any other man. She took the drink and the two strangers introduced themselves; her name was Natalie. As they talked and got to know each other, Philip began to understand his dream.

For the rest of the evening, Philip and Natalie felt a need to be with each other at all times, even when they were separated for only a few minutes. After that night, they were together always. Natalie was amazed two weeks later, when Philip told her about his dream, but both of them—even Philip, despite his devout skepticism—believe the dream is what somehow brought them together.

Philip is still a bodybuilder, still grounded and down-to-earth. But he is no longer the intractable skeptic he once was. He now knows that mysterious things sometimes happen.

One More Message from Dad

⁓

*S*USAN WAS THE kind of person whose dreams came true—literally. Once, when she dreamed that her friend cut his foot walking on the beach, her mother called a day later and said, "You know, Alan cut his foot walking on the beach." Prophetic dreams of this kind had happened on more than one occasion, so one night when Susan's deceased father came to her in a dream, she wasn't sure what to make of it.

Her father had passed away four years earlier after a long convalescence brought on by a stroke. Susan (the youngest of several children) and her mother nursed him during the last three years of his life. Even in the last year, when he could no longer speak and had to be fed through a tube, Susan spent hours with him, talking to him and telling him how much she loved him. Weakened by the stroke, her father never left his bed, and as he withdrew, Susan begged him not to leave them. When he eventually passed, her father quietly slipped away, immured in the warmth of his wife and daughter's love.

Then, after all that time, there he was again in Susan's dream. He came to her as he was before his stroke—smiling and healthy, with his trademark salt-and-pepper hair. He spoke in a soft, caring voice: "Take things more in stride, Susan. Everything will be all right." Then, there appeared, inexplicably, the face of a young man she had never seen before.

After she awoke, Susan was stumped by the vision. What was her father referring to? Was this a man she was supposed to meet? In her mid-thirties and having completed college, Susan was still single, and she was finding it harder and harder to meet men who felt right for her. She was particularly close to her mother, who was getting on in years and wanted more than anything to see her daughter settled.

Topics on love and marriage held endless interest for Susan. Several weeks after her father appeared in her dream, she decided to attend a seminar on love, dating, and marriage, hoping to learn some new approaches to romance and relationships. When the weeklong course was over, a friend she'd met there invited her and several other singles from the seminar to dinner.

The evening was pleasant enough, but after all the guests had left, Susan's friend pulled her aside and remarked, "Susan, didn't you see? Eric, the guy with the dark, curly hair was staring at you all through dinner."

"I didn't notice anyone staring at me."

"Eric is the same guy who sat next to you in the seminar last week," her friend added.

How strange, Susan thought, I don't recall that either. It seemed odd that she wouldn't have noticed the person sitting next to her, but she didn't dwell on it.

A few days later, the seminar promoters gave a party to mark the end of the course. As Susan mingled with the other party-goers, she spotted a strange man and gasped. She looked hard at him to make sure it was true, but there was no mistaking it: He was the man in the dream with her father a few weeks before. And, she found out later, he was also the man with the dark, curly hair who had watched her during her friend's dinner party and sat next to her during the course.

This time Eric approached her, formally introduced himself, and struck up a conversation. He was captivated by Susan, and at the end of the evening, he offered to drive her home. Eric worked not too far from where she lived, and a couple of days later, he showed up on her doorstep unannounced.

After Susan and Eric had gone out a couple of times, Susan's mother called.

"Your father came to me in a dream last night," her mother explained excitedly. She explained that he had appeared to her, too, as his younger self, healthy and with salt-and-pepper hair. "In my dream, he gave me a gift of some kind and told me to guard it carefully. That it was precious." Her mother paused as if she were seeing the dream again and deciphering its meaning anew. "I believe the gift is the young man you are dating. I think, Susan, your father was trying to tell me that you'll be getting married."

That's when Susan knew for sure what her father had been trying to tell her: not to worry, she would soon be getting married to this man.

Susan and Eric continued to date, and not too long afterward they were engaged to be married.

Today, Susan raises their children while Eric continues to work as an accountant, and every now and then, Susan has another, particularly vivid dream. . . .

A Grandmother's Blessing

$\sim$

IDA'S GRANDMOTHER BLESSED her every day. "Ida," she would say, "may your life be full. With good things and with children of your blood." She often used expressions from the old country. Ida would nod in agreement, mostly to please her grandmother. But as she grew older, Ida began to wonder if the blessing would ever come true.

Ida, the only daughter in a family of six children, grew up during the 1920s. Her parents had immigrated to Boston from Eastern Europe, hoping to escape the poverty and oppression they had known in their homeland. But life in America was a struggle. Her father, a kind, gentle man, owned a produce market in the working-class section of Boston's north end. But his lack of business sense kept him from turning a profit: He often paid the same bills twice because he never kept a record of his payments.

Ida's mother, a ravishing redhead who could have had her pick of husbands, had married Ida's father out of gratitude for paying her ship's passage to America. She was forced to help her husband with the business lest he drive it completely into the ground. But she despised their poverty and became a bitter, unhappy woman, often taking her disappointment out on the rest of the family.

When the Great Depression arrived in 1929, just feeding and clothing one's family was, for many, a daily effort of strength and courage. Ida scrounged for any kind of work. Then, in 1931, her grandmother became bedridden, and the task of caring for her fell upon Ida, who was then twenty-three years old. Her grandmother was already blind and frail, and once she took to her bed, she would never rise from it again.

Ida did not mind taking on this task. After all, she had worked since she was eight, when she ran an umbrella stand at Revere Beach. She was short, sturdy, and bosomy with unremarkable dark eyes and hair. She was kind and nurturing, like her father, but also practical and efficient—qualities deepened by a hard life and an unforgiving mother. For eight years, Ida tended to her grandmother faithfully—washing her, feeding her, reading to her—all the while watching her five brothers come and go, at first bringing their dates, and then later their wives and children.

From time to time, a young man would come to call on her, but once he saw how devoted Ida was to her grandmother, he would quietly make his exit. "I didn't want him anyway," Ida would say when he was gone, careful not to build up false hope. "He's not kind," she might add. But she also knew it was not in these young men to start a new life with a greater burden than they could handle.

Whenever an old friend stopped by to visit Ida's grandmother, Ida would make tea and sit watchfully by. Her grandmother always praised her: "I've been in this bed for seven years and I've never had one bed sore, so good my Ida takes care of me." She would bless Ida with the usual benediction, gazing up with pale, otherworldly eyes. Her old friends would nod in appreciation at such a devoted grandchild.

Ida's father passed away in 1937; her grandmother followed in 1939. Ida was thirty-one. She still wore her hair in a short bob—a style that had been popular in the 1920s, one that she would wear for the rest of her life. Her family was still miserably poor, and she realized it was probably too late for her to marry. By the standards of the day, she was nearly an old maid. She had neither her mother's beauty nor her charm. And now, Ida thought, she no longer had even her youth to offer. The glory of her life's accomplishments would only be known by a handful of old ladies who had visited her grandmother in that small room.

Two months after her grandmother passed, Ida had a peculiar dream. Her father came to her and said, "Go over to Mrs. Gordon's house. She has fallen and broken her leg." Ida awoke not knowing what to think. She had never dreamed anything worth remembering. And she didn't know what to make of the dream's explicit message. She decided to follow her father's advice.

The next day Ida took the bus across town to visit Mrs. Gordon, an old friend of the family. She had not seen Mrs. Gordon for a very long time, and she wondered what they would talk about. When she arrived, she found Mrs. Gordon sitting on the sofa, with a cast on her leg. The old woman greeted her warmly and explained, "The other day, I fell and broke my leg. It must be my age."

It was exactly as her father described in her dream.

Clasping her fist to her chest, Ida could only mutter, "Oh my." She was shaken. Ida was neither religious nor superstitious, and she had never heard of or experienced anything like this. Unnerved, she scanned the room to make sure it held no other surprises. Standing quietly on the far side of the room was a man. Their eyes locked, and Ida, startled, teetered back a step. Then she realized it was Murray Allen, whose family she had known when she was growing up.

"Do you know Murray, dear?" said Mrs. Gordon from the sofa. "He's one of the Allen boys."

Ida scrutinized him more closely. He was small and very thin, but he had a handsome crown of black curly hair. He said nothing, and she got the feeling that if it were not for Mrs. Gordon, he would probably keep silent. Ida had been introduced to Murray's brother ten years before, but nothing had come of it. Murray was the youngest of the brothers, and he was three years younger than Ida.

"Oh yes," Ida said. "But it has been such a long time since I've seen any of them. How do you do?"

Ida and Murray spoke a while in Mrs. Gordon's apartment. He told her he was working as a salesman. Ida's unaffected, kind demeanor put Murray at ease. A day later, he called on her.

After they had courted for several weeks, Ida still had not revealed her age. She desperately wanted to get married, and she feared that if he knew she was a few years older than he, he would not marry her, such were the conventions of the times. So Ida allowed herself this one deception and kept her true age from Murray for more than thirty years.

It would not have mattered to Murray, for he was just as happy and grateful to find her as she him. His birth had been an accident, and his harsh, disapproving father had always viewed him as just one more mouth to feed. Ida—big-hearted, kind, and nurturing—was more than Murray had ever wished for.

In 1940, Murray and Ida wed. They were devoted to each other for forty-seven years, until Ida passed away in 1987. In that time, Murray had started his own successful business, and Ida had raised four children, all from her blood.

PART THREE

Second Chances

WE *all like second chances, especially in relationships. Sometimes we meet someone, become attracted, and for a variety of reasons it doesn't work out—we're too young, not ready, or circumstances drive us apart. Sometimes our first meeting is nothing more than a brief, unremarkable encounter on our way to somewhere else. But the person sticks in our minds for months or even years afterward, and we wonder, what if. . . .*

These are stories in which two people get that second chance. They are especially moving because we feel the hand of a spiritual guiding force bridging great spans of time and circumstance to bring each couple together. We come away with a sense that when two people are meant for each other, things have a way of working out.

Valerie Takes a Holiday

$\sim$

I T WAS 1967, and Valerie was about to embark on an international adventure. She was twenty years old and had never left her native New Zealand, but she had dreamed since she was a little girl of traveling to London. She bought an open-ended ticket, not sure when she'd return home. At Auckland International Airport, she kissed her parents good-bye and boarded the plane, ready to experience the world.

Valerie got settled in London quickly, finding a job and an apartment right away. For the next two years, she soaked up the city's bustle and high energy, frequenting the street-corner pubs like any young Londoner and taking in the opera or a play when her budget allowed. She also took short trips to nearby cities and countries.

During her second summer there, Valerie's parents telephoned to say they would be taking a holiday in Spain. After hanging up the phone, Valerie thought, Why don't I surprise them with a visit? The next day, she rushed out to book the most inexpensive student-charter flight to Madrid she could find.

The day of her flight was hot by London standards. She threw on a flowered sundress, packed a small bag, and headed to Heathrow. Once she was settled into her seat, she had a craving for a cold soda. The stewardess handed her a cola, and Valerie held out her money to pay.

"I'm sorry," the stewardess said, "we only accept Spanish pesetas."

"Oh, but I've only got English pence," Valerie stammered. She looked through her purse in vain. In her rush to make the trip, she hadn't had time to exchange any English pounds for Spanish money.

A young man sitting across the aisle intervened. "Not to worry," he said, reaching into his pocket. "I've got pesetas." His accent was Australian.

He handed the stewardess the money and smiled at Valerie—a roguish grin that lit up the whole airplane and which, Valerie noted throughout the flight, he used often.

"Thank you," Valerie said gratefully.

"Where are you from?" he asked.

"New Zealand."

"A kiwi. We're neighbors then." He flashed his generous smile again, and his deep tan made his teeth look especially white.

They exchanged a few more pleasantries and some travel tips—two strangers sharing a momentary intimacy simply because they're together in a country not their own.

Later, standing in the queue at Spanish customs, Valerie admired the Australian's deft handling of the agent's questions. He must travel all the time, she guessed. Before dashing off to a connecting flight, he smiled at her and waved good-bye.

AFTER SURPRISING her parents in Spain, Valerie returned to London, where she stayed for six more months. By that time she felt she was ready to return to Auckland. She had been away from home for two and half years. She missed her family and had had her fill of travel.

After several weeks back in New Zealand, Valerie and her brother met some friends for dinner at a hotel. At one point during the meal, three young men entered the dining room and headed toward the bar. Some diners looked up momentarily from their plates to notice the men's arrival. Not recognizing the new faces, they resumed their dinner conversations. But Valerie's concentration was broken: One of the men looked *so* familiar. Where on earth do I know him from? she wondered. She couldn't place him, and she decided she had to get a closer look.

Valerie approached the bar on the pretext of ordering a drink, slipping sidelong glances at the one who looked familiar.

"You're wearing the same thing you wore on the flight to Spain," he said, turning to her suddenly and smiling broadly. She glanced down at her flowered sundress, then her eyes widened. Of course! She'd never forget that smile.

"You're the man who paid for my drink on the plane! The one to Spain!" she said excitedly. "This is quite a coincidence!"

This time they introduced themselves.

David was twenty-two, and he had been traveling around the world for six years since his father's untimely death. He was about to return to his job in Spain working for a professor at an archaeological expedition in Majorca.

"I'm staying with some friends on Spruce Street," he told her.

"That's just around the corner from where my parents live," Valerie said, marveling to herself at the coincidence.

During their conversation, David mentioned a television program he had heard was airing the following week: the subject was Spain, as seen through the eyes of Ernest Hemingway.

"Why don't we watch the program together?" David suggested. "It's about Spain after all."

Valerie accepted.

The night they watched the program on Spain was the first of many dates, and their romance progressed quickly after that. David quit his archaeology job, and within a few months, he and Valerie married and settled in Auckland, where they raised two children. They still live there today, though they rarely travel anymore—the only world they need to see is right at home in New Zealand.

The Keepsake

~

WHEN HE WAS a junior in high school in 1980, Ross fell in love for the first and only time.

It happened unexpectedly. Ross lived in Walnut Creek, California, a community in the San Francisco Bay Area. He had just ended things with a girlfriend, and he was in the midst of experiencing the unique misery of teenage breakup. One night Ross's friend Dean asked Ross to go to see Dean's brother in a play at the local high school across town. Ross, wallowing in his heartache, said he didn't feel like going, but Dean persisted. To shut him up, Ross acquiesced.

At the cast party afterward, Ross stood sheepishly in a corner with his hands in his pockets. But his mood lifted considerably the moment he spotted the most beautiful girl he had ever seen. He practically bounced as he walked, making his way over to her. He introduced himself; she said her name was Debbie. They immediately hit it off.

Debbie had blond hair and large, luminous blue eyes, and she laughed at every one of his flirtatious jokes. After only a few minutes, Ross thought to himself: I can't believe this. She's incredible. She's smart, she's funny, she's pretty—man, she's everything. Ross was buoyant.

Dean was ready to leave.

"In a minute," Ross said. He turned back to Debbie.

"Hey, let's go," Dean pressed. But after half an hour of waiting, Dean left without him. Ross didn't care: He and Debbie stayed, talking and laughing together.

Later in the evening, Ross asked for her telephone number.

"I don't know . . . I don't think it's a good idea," Debbie said. Ross was crushed. He wondered if he had misread the signals. Eventually, he got a ride home from someone at the party.

The next day, Ross was determined to get Debbie's phone number. But Dean's brother couldn't help him, and her home number was unlisted. Ross grew antsy. He found a doctor's office listing under Debbie's last name. But even before he was able to try that number, his phone rang during dinner that evening. His mom answered.

"It's someone named Debbie," she said, looking at Ross. He could barely swallow the bite of food he had been chewing.

"Tell her I'll call her back," he said, half rising from the table. He tried to sound calm and hoped no one would notice the tiny beads of nervous sweat breaking out on his forehead.

After dinner, he grabbed a pen and paper and jotted down several topics they could talk about. Later, he found out she had done the same thing. But they talked that evening for a long time—without referring to their lists.

"Hey, how come you didn't want to give me your phone number?" Ross asked before they hung up.

"I don't know. No one has ever asked for my phone number before. I guess I didn't know what to do."

She's amazing, Ross thought after they said good-bye.

After their first date they were inseparable. They spent almost every waking moment together—the way most couples do when they're seventeen and in love. Debbie's was the best kind of companionship, Ross thought: fun-loving, sensitive, and not overly emotional. Her presence alone made him feel more comfortable in the world, more masculine, and she inspired in him something he hadn't felt before: a desire for romance. After their first kiss, Ross said, "You make me feel like Captain Kirk."

"Captain Kirk?" Debbie asked, laughing.

"Yeah. Captain Kirk on *Star Trek* kissing some beautiful alien woman." Debbie laughed again.

Debbie was a senior, a year ahead of Ross. They passed a tender, magical summer together before Debbie was to head down to college at the University of California at Los Angeles. The last days were excruciating for Ross; all he could think about was that soon she would be gone. One cool night toward the end of summer, Ross said to Debbie, "I want to marry you. I can't imagine anything better than coming home to you every night."

"Oh Ross, that's so sweet," Debbie said. But they both knew they were too young for marriage—they had too much yet to see and do. Ross had expressed a loving sentiment more than anything else, and they were about to part ways, possibly forever. In fact, it would be a long time before they had another night like this. But the night sky would not forget his words, the stars holding them in their shimmering net for safe-keeping.

Ross spent his senior year in high school in a daze of longing for Debbie. A couple of times, he drove down to Los Angeles to see her, telling his parents he was visiting his sister at San Diego State. But on these visits, Debbie seemed distracted. When they talked on the phone, she was distant. Then, after a while, Debbie told him that they should probably not go out anymore. Their relationship wasn't going anywhere, and besides, she was in college.

"It's time we should be doing our own thing," Debbie said.

Ross was devastated.

He had always planned to go to the University of California at Berkeley—his father had pressed him to go there—but during his senior year, Ross had applied to UCLA to be with Debbie. Now, even before he had received his acceptance letter, Debbie had broken up with him. That fall, Ross went to UCLA anyway.

They didn't get back together when he arrived on campus, though from time to time, he and Debbie crossed paths. They would chat casually, and Ross's heart would ache to see her beautiful smile, her huge blue eyes, and the way she laughed at even his smallest quip. She's moved on, he thought. I guess I'll have to do the same.

Time slipped by. Debbie graduated and moved to Long Beach, near Los Angeles. Ross attended law school in San Francisco. He would call her on her birthday, and each time Ross would hang up thinking: We get along so well. Why aren't we together?

Ross was maturing into an attractive young man. He was

tall and well-built, with a strong, chiseled face and pale blue eyes that pulled downward at the edges. He was popular, easy-going, and always ready with a wisecrack. He had a wide circle of friends and he dated often, but he invariably compared every girl he went out with to Debbie. He couldn't help himself. Though he dated, hoping to meet a woman he could spend his life with, he couldn't shake the feeling that he already had.

Ross returned to Los Angeles after graduating from law school to work for a large downtown firm. When he decided his temperament was not well suited for the law, he took a job at a local pharmaceutical company.

Once, in 1988, Ross and Debbie ran into each other back home in Walnut Creek. In minutes it was just like old times. Ross charmed Debbie, who laughed heartily and matched his wit. Later, Debbie told her mom about running into Ross. Debbie looked so despondent for a moment that her mom asked, "Do you still have feelings for Ross?"

Ross? Debbie thought silently. But she didn't answer.

Four years passed. Debbie had gotten into a serious relationship with another guy, and Ross was also in a serious relationship—he and Elise had been together for three and half years, and they were talking about marriage. Elise had just gone to Europe on vacation with her family for a couple of weeks, leaving Ross on his own. Not having much to do, he decided to call Debbie, thinking it would be great to see an old friend. Debbie answered on the first ring. Her boyfriend was also out of town that week.

They met at a popular seafood restaurant by the beach. The night was cool and damp along the coast; the sky was clear and crowded with stars. Over white wine and grilled fish, they caught up on the last few years of their lives. Ross was in fine form, and Debbie laughed so hard she had to hold on to her sides. Sparks were flying between them.

After a while, Debbie said, "I've been seeing someone for six months now. It's pretty serious."

"Yeah?" Ross said. He looked down at his plate.

"Yep. I think this might be it." Debbie took a sip of wine. She looked up at him. "What about you and Elise? Are you guys still together?" Ross felt his stomach tighten.

"Yeah. Still together. We're going on four years now. She's really great."

"Uh-huh."

"We're actually in couples counseling. You know, iron a few things out, if we're going to get married. She really wants to get married."

"That seems like a good idea. I'm really happy for you."

"Yeah, me too. I mean, I'm happy for you, too." There was, for the first time, an awkward pause in their conversation.

The topic switched to old times. With their conversation, the stars' net loosened, and a moody nostalgia floated above their table.

Finally, Debbie asked, "Remember the first time we kissed? You told me I made you feel like Captain Kirk."

"Captain Kirk! I said that?" Ross hid his face for a moment. He dropped his hands and looked at her. "You know, you're the *only* girl who ever made me feel like Captain Kirk."

Then his tone softened and he became serious.

"Debbie," he said, opening up his heart to her, "I can't marry Elise. I could never marry her. For God's sake, we're in couples counseling and we're not even engaged. I tried to make it work, but—there was always you. There has only been you."

"Oh Ross—"

"You're the only one who understands my jokes."

"Well, you're funny, Ross. You are really funny."

That night, despite the seriousness of the relationships they were already in, they decided they would give themselves another chance.

Debbie was thirty. She'd seen what she'd wanted to see of the world, and for her as well, no one else had made her feel so comfortable. She had come back to Ross, and incredibly, they had both grown up to become adults and yet the love from their teenage years remained.

To Ross, it was a miracle that Debbie was still single. He had been so afraid that he would call one year and she would tell him that she was engaged. He told her later that every time he saw her through the years he would think, That face, that face is for me.

And so, twelve years after they had first met, Debbie and Ross became inseparable—again. They became engaged a few months later and married in 1994. Today, they both work for the same pharmaceutical company and live in L.A. with their daughter, who has the same big, blue eyes as her mother. It's a dream come true for Ross, who now comes home to two smiling faces each night.

The Second Blind Date

⁓

IN 1989, ALAN was in his last year of medical school at Northwestern University in Chicago. Before he started the arduous, nationwide application process to find a college that would host his residency in internal medicine, he took a short vacation to Los Angeles. He stayed with his cousin Joanne and made plans to meet an ex-girlfriend one Saturday night. When Alan's plans fell through, Joanne came up with another suggestion.

"I know someone nice who's at USC medical school. Maybe you'd like to meet her," Joanne said. "Her name is Eileen."

With nothing else to do, Alan agreed.

They met for dinner at an old-style Italian restaurant and talked easily all through the evening. Eileen had a soft, distracted quality, and Alan liked her right away. She sometimes mumbled the last few words of her sentences so that he had to lean closer to hear her. At one point she mentioned she had family in Chicago and was planning a trip there in a couple of weeks, so when Alan dropped her off, he said, "Why don't you call me when you're in Chicago?"

"Sure," Eileen said.

But Eileen never called. Each day, Alan waited to hear from her; she had made an impression on him, and he thought they could really hit it off if they had the chance. But he had miscalculated: She was not the type to call a man, no matter what the circumstances.

Alan mentioned his blind date to his best friend, Dan, openly wondering if Eileen might not be the kind of woman he had always hoped to meet. Months passed, however, and Alan became absorbed in the application process for medical residency programs. He was having a hard time deciding which school he wanted to go to—Harvard, his true first choice, or several others, including University of California at Los Angeles.

"UCLA is a great school. It has a lot going for it," Dan said one night with several other friends over beers.

"Yeah. The best-looking girls are in L.A.," another friend threw in.

"But its internal medicine program doesn't rate," Alan countered.

"Come on, Alan, *Eileen* lives in L.A.," Dan said, chiding him. Alan smiled—was he crazy to have gotten so excited over a single blind date?

In the end, Alan got into Harvard, and he moved to Boston that fall.

Alan's residency was grueling, and he often pulled hundred-hour weeks in the hospital. He met another doctor, and after dating for three years, they became engaged. But Alan could not settle on a date for the wedding; something didn't feel right. Eventually, he realized the engagement was a mistake and broke it off.

Afterward, Alan continued to date. Every once in a while Eileen would pop into his head. He didn't exactly pine away for her; after all, they only had one date. But he never quite forgot her either, and he would sometimes wonder what she was up to. After a particularly dismal date, the thought would sometimes cross his mind, What if I hadn't gotten into Harvard? What if I had gone to UCLA?

Upon finishing his residency, Alan got a job working in a practice in Brookline, Massachusetts. One evening, in the fall of 1995, he got a phone message from his cousin Joanne. He had not talked to her for more than two years.

"I have someone to fix you up with," Joanne's voice said on the machine. "I assume you're still single since I haven't gotten any wedding invitations. Let me know if you want to meet her. This one is special."

A couple of days earlier, Joanne had run into an old friend at a party. They hadn't spoken for several years, and as they caught up, their conversation turned to the perils of dating.

"It's a rare event for me even to meet someone I like enough to go out with," the friend lamented.

"I've got a great cousin from Chicago you should meet," Joanne told her. "He's a doctor. I'm pretty sure he's still single. He's been living in Boston ever since he graduated from medical school. Why don't I give him a call?"

Joanne spent the next few minutes describing Alan, and her friend said, "He sounds great"—and because she would be in

Philadelphia soon to take her medical board exams, she said she could meet him while she was on the East Coast.

Alan called Joanne back to find out more about this girl she talked so highly of. Joanne began to describe her, but Alan interrupted her almost immediately: "Wait a minute. She sounds familiar. Is she that Eileen girl you once set me up with, a long time ago?"

"Yes. Her name's Eileen. Do you know her?"

"Yeah, I know her. *You* fixed me up with her when I was still in medical school. We went out on one date, in L.A., six years ago."

"I fixed you up with her? But she says she never met you."

"I'm telling you I went out with her."

"That's strange. I described you in detail to her. She has no idea who you are," Joanne said.

"How can she not remember me?"

"I don't know. You only had one date. A lot of people wouldn't remember. Anyway, do you want her number?"

Alan took her number, and then called his best friend Dan, who was also living in Boston, to get some advice.

"Should I go see her in Philadelphia?" Alan asked. "She doesn't even remember me. And I hate these long-distance things."

"You have to go, man. It's *Eileen*."

So Alan called her. His voice did not trigger her memory as he had hoped.

"It was 1989," Alan said. "We went to Westwood. We ate dinner in an Italian restaurant."

"I don't remember," Eileen said. "It was just one date."

"We wanted to see a movie. But it was sold out. So we walked around for an hour. You wanted frozen yogurt—chocolate."

"Alan," Eileen said soothingly, "it's nothing to get upset about. I'll go out with you."

Alan flew to Philadelphia to see Eileen, and they spent the entire day together. She was exactly as he had remembered: soft, demure, and still clumsily mumbling off the end of her sentences. It was as if they had just shared that Italian dinner last week. And this time Eileen felt the same connection and desire that Alan did—it seemed impossible that six years had passed between meetings. They rose above the reign of time's measured pace, and long stretches of years fell away before a single moment.

Eileen returned to L.A., but they continued to get to know each other, talking almost every single day. Alan began looking for any excuse to fly there, and he found one four months later: His alma mater, Northwestern's football team, was going to play the USC Trojans—Eileen's old college—in the 1996 Rose Bowl in Los Angeles. Alan invited Eileen to the game, bought two tickets, and flew across the country to meet her.

The day of the game, the stadium was packed, and all afternoon the teams fought tooth-and-nail, neither side able to take a commanding lead in the high-scoring contest. Each team's fans rose to their feet with a resounding cheer at every score by their side. Toward the end, USC scored a spectacular touchdown and the crowd went crazy, cheering wildly. When the din quieted, Alan turned to Eileen and said, "If USC wins, will you marry me?" She just laughed. But then she said, "Okay."

Northwestern didn't score again, and with that, Alan and Eileen were engaged. They were married in the early spring of 1996 and now live in Brookline, where they are raising their family and practicing medicine.

The Farm

⁓

In 1932, THE young coeds at Stanford University called it
the Farm. Once home to several thousand Stanford students, it
was actually a cluster of Spanish-style buildings at the base of
the foothills of California's Santa Cruz Mountains.

Mary, who could trace her family's roots in California long
before the Gold Rush, was smart, ambitious, and eager to make
her mark in the world in a way that was still rare for women at
that time. Just passing Stanford's stiff admission's standards—
not to mention its enrollment limit of only five hundred
women—was achievement enough, but Mary wanted much
more. Her interests were varied and passionate: writing,
archaeology, drama. She performed regularly at the "Gaieties,"
shows put on by students the night before the "Big Game" (the
annual football contest pitting Stanford against its archrival
Cal, the University of California at Berkeley).

When Carl first saw Mary, she was a freshman marching
across fraternity row, her face knitted in an intense expression,
her arms clutching a stack of books tightly to her chest. She was

tall and slim, with long, thick black hair, and she wore a long beige skirt and a white blouse. The fraternity boys hollered and hooted, as they did at all the passing girls, but Mary strode by without a glance, oblivious to the catcalls.

Two weeks later, the freshman dorm, Roble Hall, hosted a "jolly-up," one of their occasional dances, and Mary stood around feeling rather silly as she waited for someone to ask her to dance. A dark-haired man stepped forward and swirled her onto the dance floor. After the band bellowed a few notes from "Blue Moon," Carl approached them and tapped Mary's partner on the shoulder.

"May I have this dance?" he asked, breaking in gently.

Mary was stunned. An upperclassman, tall, wide-shouldered, blond, and tan, Carl was the most beautiful man she had ever seen—and she would have been even more stunned if she'd known that the only reason he'd come was to see her. Fascinated by his vision of the rather mysterious Mary, Carl had discovered that she lived at Roble Hall—and took a chance that she would attend the event. For the rest of the night they danced the fox-trot and the waltz, and no one dared break their hold.

After that night, Carl and Mary spent two inseparable years together, enclosed by their love and the gently sloping foothills of the Farm. Carl, who had acquired his looks and good manners from his Swedish-born parents, always wore a jacket on a date even when they only went for ice cream at Sticky Wilson's. He kissed her when he dropped her off at her dorm each night, but he never dared venture past the door's threshold. They became something of an item on campus. They were easily spotted driving around in his red Buick roadster: Carl's shock of blond hair and Mary's black tresses blowing loose from the scarf she fastened under her chin.

Despite their seemingly carefree days, the Great Depression seeped into the privileged environs of Stanford. After the presidential elections in 1932, Mary and Carl, along with hundreds of others, waved to Herbert Hoover, who had come outside for a moment on the lawn of his nearby Palo Alto home to address his supporters. He had just lost the race to Franklin Delano Roosevelt, the president who would eventually deliver the country from poverty and into a new era.

The impact of the Depression and Mary's fierce ambition drove her to work hard in college; her dream was to write scripts for the silver screen in Hollywood. Her aunt, a prolific and well-known Hollywood writer, was her inspiration and mentor, and Mary planned to follow in her footsteps.

Carl's future plans were less certain, for he felt no driving ambition or direction. He was a gifted artist, something of a rebel, and spoiled even by his own admission, and he resisted his mother's desire that he take after his parents and work in a bank. After he graduated from college, Carl bummed around Los Angeles—a city his mother disapproved of—taking odd jobs and painting a great deal.

When Mary talked to her father about Carl and the possibility that they might get married, her father would ask, "How are you going to make a living?" The question took on greater poignancy as the Depression continued. Despite their love, Carl and Mary could not resolve the differences in their professional and personal desires, and they eventually broke off their relationship.

After graduating, Mary headed south to Los Angeles to the world-famous film studio MGM (Metro Goldwyn Mayer) to work in the publicity department and learn all she could about film. Carl remained in Northern California, eventually joining the Army Air Corps as the country prepared to enter World War II. By then, Mary and Carl had lost touch.

Mary wrote voraciously, and like her aunt, she became a prolific and successful screenwriter. She married her writing partner from the studio, and together they wrote a number of popular films. In all, eighteen of her scripts were made into movies, including *Gentlemen Marry Brunettes,* Mary's response to her aunt's enormously popular *Gentlemen Prefer Blondes.* She had a son, traveled, wrote books, and pursued her passion for archaeology. Her life was rich with friends and work. But in the end, her marriage did not work out, and she and her husband separated.

Meanwhile, Carl became a pilot and was stationed in England during World War II. He met and married a woman there, and they eventually returned to Monterey in Northern California. Carl opened a successful ceramics business, and he was able to support his growing family. He thought of Mary from time to time, particularly after seeing her name on a screenplay credit—remembering the way he first saw her marching down fraternity row, so determined and driven. He'd shake his head, and the memory—which brought a smile— always left him feeling a bit empty; no one else had been quite like her.

SEVERAL DECADES passed. It was 1989, and Mary, long separated from her ex-husband, accepted a friend's offer to write and stay at his ranch, which claimed several of the most beautiful acres in Paso Robles. Mary longed to be in Northern California again and to see the wild poppies that colored the landscape a brilliant orange every spring. The ranch, though beautiful, was quiet and isolated, and her writing was more solemn than usual.

One morning, after the fog had lifted to reveal a perfect spring day, Mary suggested to her friend that they go have lunch in nearby Monterey. It was a lovely afternoon as they drove the windy roads of Carmel Valley, but after a few too many unfamiliar turns, they realized they were lost. They kept driving up into the hills passing lovely, gracious old homes, while Mary gazed out of the window. As they drove along Gentry Hill, she spotted a residential signpost with a name that startled her: it was Carl's. She stared at it silently, thinking *That's the man I should have married.*

After she returned home to Santa Monica in Los Angeles, she could think of nothing else. Memories of Stanford came flooding back: Carl with his glorious blond hair, their talks late into the evening, their carefree rides around campus in his red Buick roadster. They hadn't seen each other in fifty-five years. A surge of sadness tightened her heart. Some things could not be undone. She imagined his life with a wife and children, and thought for a moment that it would be better not to intrude. But after a few days, she called anyway.

A woman's voice answered. Mary cautiously addressed her as Carl's wife.

"No, I'm the housekeeper. I'm afraid Carl's wife passed away a few months ago."

"A few months ago?"

"Yes."

"Well, tell Carl an old friend called—Mary." She hung up the phone, her hands shaking.

When Carl got the message, he was out feeding his horses. Later, the housekeeper told Mary that in the twenty-six years she had worked for Carl, she had never seen him cry. He ran back to the house and called Mary immediately. Just the familiar sound of their voices had them chattering as excitedly as children. They agreed that she should fly back immediately.

A few days later, Carl met Mary at the Monterey airport. Mary was worried that things would be different, that he would find her changed. She was heavy now, an old woman. When she emerged from the gate, she recognized him immediately—still tall, but age had stooped his shoulders, and his skin was lined and leathery. Carl's eyes, however, were still blue and clear, and he was wearing a big felt hat with a feather in it. Their eyes met, and as they came close and embraced, they started to cry.

As they drove back to Carl's house, Mary couldn't help wondering why Carl didn't remove his large hat. Oh, he's probably bald, she thought, remembering all his lovely, blond hair. They talked, sharing their long life stories and falling into the natural rhythm that marked their conversations in college. Carl's wife had died after a long illness, and he had four grown children. He had inherited Gentry Hill, his mother's land. Their lives, comfortable and unfettered with responsibilities, were as if they had picked up where they had left off at Stanford.

When they reached Carl's house, he finally took off his hat—revealing a thick, full head of hair, now gone completely white.

"Your hair!" Mary exclaimed, "It's beautiful! Why were you wearing that hat?"

"So you would think I was still a country boy," Carl said. They both laughed.

To Carl, Mary was still the same incredible woman he had known, and this time, he would not let her get away. He asked her to marry him, which she did in 1990, fifty-eight years after their first dance at Roble Hall.

It Takes Two

⟝⟞

$\mathcal{A}$T FAIRFAX HIGH SCHOOL in Los Angeles in 1973, Guy was in the popular clique. He was charming, and his disarming manner made him a friend with everyone. Though Fairfax's student body was huge, everyone seemed to know Guy.

Dinah, however, was not part of any particular group; she just hung out with a small bunch of girlfriends. Guy and Dinah never attended the same parties or events, but they talked on several occasions, and whenever they passed in the hall, she would shyly return his friendly greeting. They never gave a thought to each other more than that, especially Guy, who was deeply in love with a girl he had known since junior high.

Dinah was a flower child, a free spirit. She wore flowing, gauzy dresses and let her hair grow long and loose. She was a liberated woman of the seventies who focused on a career and individual expression, rather than marriage, which she viewed as a suspect institution.

After graduating high school in 1973, Dinah went to college in Texas and then earned a graduate degree in nutrition.

She was still living in Texas when she received an invitation to her ten-year high school reunion. She was intrigued to find out what had become of her old classmates, but she hesitated: She would have to fly back to Los Angeles, and she hadn't exactly kept in touch with many people from high school. In the end, however, her curiosity prevailed, and she booked a flight.

The reunion was a poignant experience. Dinah ran into friends she had not thought about in a decade, and the music they played took her back to her life during the early seventies, an age that was now long gone. She hadn't expected to have such a good time, and she stayed for the entire party, reminiscing with old friends and acquaintances.

By 2 A.M., the reunion finally began to wind down, and by 3 A.M., the room was practically empty. Only a few stragglers remained. It was then that Dinah spotted Guy. She walked up behind him and tapped him on the shoulder. He turned around to find Dinah's gentle smile.

"Hey, Dinah! How've you been?" Guy asked in his typically friendly manner. "Where have you been hiding? I haven't seen you here all night."

"I've been here," she said. She looked better now than she had in high school: a lovely grown woman of twenty-seven, she still wore her hair long and loose. She was now quite poised, but she had retained a certain relaxed openness that Guy found refreshing.

"A bunch of us are going to Cantor's. Why don't you come along?" Guy said.

"Sure," Dinah replied, happy to be asked.

At Cantor's, an all-night diner that was a throwback to an

earlier era, Guy and Dinah talked more than they had during all their years in high school. An unmistakable chemistry flowed between them. When Guy drove Dinah home to her parents' house, he asked if he could come in. Dinah hesitated.

"I wouldn't want to ruin our friendship," Dinah said.

"What friendship?" Guy asked, laughing good naturedly, "We haven't seen each other in ten years." Dinah laughed too, and before he drove off, Guy said sincerely, "It's really great to see you." And with that, he left.

A couple of days later, Dinah called him from Texas. She had just broken up with her boyfriend.

"I'm sorry," she said. "I wish I would have taken you up on your offer."

They talked some more, happy to have made a connection, but that seemed to be the end of it. Dinah and Guy were both more focused on building their careers than on getting married and building a family, and so they went on with their lives. They traveled in and out of relationships, never settling down, not committing—living out another legacy of the seventies generation.

WHEN DINAH received her invitation to the Fairfax High School Class of 1973's twenty-year high school reunion, she was living in Monterey, an idyllic, seaside town in Northern California. This time she didn't hesitate to RSVP.

The party, held at the Biltmore Hotel in downtown L.A., was not quite the same as last time. Fewer alumni showed up, and most were now married with children. Things began to fizzle around midnight as the married ones rushed home to

relieve their baby-sitters. The last few stragglers, mostly singles, moved toward the hotel's entrance. Dinah spotted a friend
of Guy's.

"Where's Guy?" she asked him.

"He's around," the friend answered, searching the room.
"Go and tell him, 'Let's get naked,'" was Guy's friends's sage
advice.

Finally, they spotted Guy, and Dinah tapped him on the
shoulder from behind. They hadn't spoken since their conversation ten years earlier.

"Hey," Dinah said as he turned around, a mischievous grin
on her face. "Let's get naked."

"I don't know," Guy said, not missing a beat, "it might ruin
our friendship."

Still single, Guy and his two friends were ready to go out,
and they invited Dinah along. Just then, the class president
rushed over. His wife worked for Los Angeles mayor Tom
Bradley, who had given her a complimentary voucher for a
night's stay in the Biltmore's Presidential Suite.

"My wife had to go out of town on business at the last
minute," he said. "I hate to see this room go to waste. Why
don't you guys take it." The suite, which occupied half the
floor, cost more than a thousand dollars a night. They all went
up to see it, but Guy's friends soon exited discreetly, leaving
Guy and Dinah alone.

They spent the night in the palatial suite, talking till dawn
and watching the sun rise over the City of Angels. It was magical. Dinah—mature, nearing forty, but still a flower child at
heart—was a breath of fresh air to Guy, who had recently

ended a difficult relationship with a very serious and intense woman.

That night, Dinah invited Guy to visit her in Monterey. He did so the next weekend—and for many weekends after that. When Guy mentioned to another old high school friend that he was seeing Dinah, the friend was surprised.

"Really?" his friend said. "You'll never get her. She's such a free spirit."

But in truth, Dinah was tired of being alone. She was tired of men in and out of her life, and she yearned for the comfort and commitment of marriage.

And they still didn't rush to the altar: It took them three more years. When they finally did marry in 1997, he at forty-two and she at forty, it was the first time for both of them.

Vision of the Heart

⌒

IN 1951, MARY ANN was attending a nursing program at New York University offered in conjunction with Bellevue Hospital. She had recently transferred from Mount Saint Mary, a small, elite, Catholic women's college in upstate New York. A large, kind woman, Mary Ann had spent her freshman year at St. Mary's dreaming about becoming a nun—instead of studying for her medical degree—and her mother had quickly put a stop to it. Forceful and domineering, and not giving her daughter any choice in the matter, her mother made her switch to NYU and give up her religious aspirations to learn a practical profession.

One day one of her classmates at NYU asked Mary Ann if she would be interested in becoming a reader for the classmate's blind brother, Gene, and Mary Ann jumped at the idea. Gene was a graduate music student at Columbia University, and Mary Ann scheduled to go for a few hours three times a week and read to him from music texts.

Gene, a first generation Italian American, was a dark-haired, intelligent young man with a powerful physique—the result of years of competitive wrestling with a blind wrestling team. Gene was born in New York City only a few months after his parents had emigrated from a small seaside village along Italy's Adriatic Coast: He was a perfect baby, with a shock of black hair and striking indigo eyes. But at two and a half, Gene contracted measles, and the doctor inserted an overly potent solution of silver nitrate into his eyes to prevent infection. The burning solution severed his optical and olfactory nerves, and he would never see nor smell again. His dark blue irises turned opaque.

Growing up, Gene attended schools for the blind. In high school, Gene headed an especially talented group of blind wrestlers, who won several state championships competing against sighted teams, and Gene and another teammate went on to compete nationally. Gene's success in wrestling gave him the confidence to attend Columbia. He took a certain pride in the fact that he never carried a cane when he walked. At first glance, you would never have known he was blind.

The first night Mary Ann was to read to Gene, she rode the subway for an hour and fifteen minutes from Bellevue Hospital and then carefully checked the numbers on the two-story brownstones on Gene's block, searching for his home. Shivering from the cold, she headed up the stairs and knocked softly on his door.

"Come in," Gene said. "Did you find my apartment all right?"

"Yes. Thank you."

Mary Ann entered Gene's tiny, one-room apartment, which

was completely dark except for the streetlight coming through a single window.

"Do you mind if I turn on the light?" she asked politely.

"How else can you read?" he replied, smiling. He turned in her direction. "I think we've met somewhere before."

"I don't know. I don't think so," she answered, considering it.

"It was at my sister's. She had a dinner party." He was right; Gene's sister was also a nursing student, and she had invited Mary Ann over one evening. Gene remembered her voice, which sounded unusually shy and self-conscious; Mary Ann spoke only when spoken to.

Gene had developed a keen sensitivity to people's voices—their pitch and tone, from which he discerned much about the kindness or coldness of the speaker's nature—and he himself was very articulate. He chose his words thoughtfully, deliberately, and spoke in a measured, musical rhythm. Voices and words and music were his great pleasures, and within them lived vivid worlds of love and destruction.

"What shall we start with?" Mary Ann asked, sifting through the stack of heavy books.

"How about the romantic composers?"

She shuffled through the books, unable to locate the title. "It's second from the bottom," he said. She pulled out the book.

"From the beginning?"

"Yes."

She sat down and began to read. Her voice was high-pitched, feminine, and soft, revealing a caring but timid nature, the product of a sheltered life. While reading, she never rushed or grew impatient, even toward the end of the evening as she faced the long train ride home to Bellevue. Every so often she stopped to rest, and they talked a bit. Then she would begin again, the gentle modulation of her voice enclosing them in a rarefied peace.

She returned nearly every other night over the next few weeks. The evenings took on their own sweet cadence—filled with the warm sound of her voice in the small room—and the imperceptible spaces between each word took on their own significance, filling up with thoughts and feelings, first of friendship, then of love.

Soon, Gene found himself waiting impatiently for each reading, and he pursued her the way he had never pursued any woman. They began to date, and by bus or train, he would take her back to Bellevue at evening's end. They attended Columbia football games in the rain, huddled under an umbrella; they ate in Central Park or strolled, arm in arm, along the shops on Fifth Avenue. Gene sometimes purchased student tickets for the Metropolitan Opera, where they would sit in the seats farthest from the stage, surrounded by other music majors and aspiring composers as Madame Butterfly sang about heartbreak and lost love. At times, Mary Ann would forget entirely that Gene was blind, so smoothly and comfortably did they move through the world together. In just three months, Gene and Mary Ann began to talk about getting married.

But Mary Ann's mother, an iron-willed Irish matron, disapproved of Gene, whose aspirations and imagined potential did not match what she had in mind for her daughter. Born into a comfortable Irish family—the only daughter among five sons—Mary Ann's mother was spoiled as a child, and she married a man who lavished her with attention and deferred to her every desire.

"If you are not going to be a doctor, at least marry one," her mother told her with finality.

Timid and retiring, Mary Ann acquiesced, as she always had. She depended on her parents for financial support, and she was no match for her mother when they disagreed. Her mother didn't like any of the other men who soon came to take Mary Ann out either, but she would say, "At least they will take her mind off Gene."

Mary Ann stopped seeing Gene. Too afraid and embarrassed to explain the reason why, she simply never returned and never called. She knew he would fight her, and worse yet, she could not bear to see her cowardice reflected in his face.

Gene called her house, but Mary Ann would not talk to him. He tried calling her at Bellevue.

"I'm sorry, Gene," said another nursing student. "She says she can't come to the phone."

Heartbroken and confused, Gene rode the bus to Bellevue to find her, but she refused to see him. She could walk right past me and I wouldn't even know it, Gene thought miserably. Eventually, he gave up and stopped calling.

For weeks he stayed home alone and refused to go out, mourning the loss of Mary Ann's sweet spirit.

Weeks became months, and Gene slowly became reconnected with the world as he came to terms with his despair and anger over losing Mary Ann. Eventually, he met another woman, and after a couple of years, they became engaged.

Mary Ann thought about Gene every day during this time.

One afternoon, a moment of courage swept over her and she scribbled him a note.

> *Dear Gene,*
>
> *I miss you more than I can say. I don't care what my mother wants. I want to marry you, if you will still have me. We'll elope if we have to. I'm sorry for the pain I've caused. Please forgive me. I will never leave you again.*
>
> *Love,*
> *Mary Ann*

She quickly sealed the envelope and rushed the letter to the post office before she could change her mind.

A couple of days later, Gene's fiancée was gathering Gene's mail in order to read it to him, and she came across Mary Ann's letter. Alone, she opened the letter and read it to herself, then she tore it up and never said a word to Gene.

Mary Ann waited anxiously for a response. When it never came, she sadly thought, This serves me right! I was cruel to leave him, and now he wants nothing to do with me.

A few months later, Gene's sister—Mary Ann's former classmate—sent Mary Ann an invitation to Gene's wedding. Against her better judgment, Mary Ann decided to attend. She sat in the back of the Catholic Church and did not try to approach or talk to Gene. A hard rain fell outside as everyone waited for the wedding procession, but Mary Ann couldn't bear it. As the organ music started and the ceremony began, Mary Ann rose and fled the church in tears.

Gene was married for nineteen years. He and his wife raised two children, but it was not a happy marriage. For extra money, Gene played piano for a jazz band, the Mood Men. For fifteen years, the band played in clubs all over Connecticut, New York, and New Jersey. He played with passion and feeling, and his music helped him get through the hard times. For two years, the band played at Ricardo's, a popular restaurant and nightclub in Queens. Strangely enough, Mary Ann—who lived in New York City at the time—frequented the restaurant, but she never saw Gene's band.

Through the years, Gene often thought of Mary Ann. Once, he even tried to contact her again, calling her mother's house.

"The Myrons have moved upstate," her mother said.

"She's married?" Gene asked.

"Yes," Her mother replied.

Mary Ann married a fellow nursing student from Bellevue. They had a daughter, and when her husband decided to go to medical school, Mary Ann supported him. But once he earned his medical degree, he left them and moved to California. Afterward, Mary Ann moved with her daughter to Glen Falls, New York, a quiet town in the foothills of the Adirondack Mountains, where she worked as a nurse in the intensive care unit at the local hospital.

IN 1975, Gene divorced his wife, and with his children now grown, he decided to find Mary Ann, propelled by the conviction that something remained unfinished between them. He called her mother's house, but the family had moved and left no forwarding address. He tried Bellevue Hospital, but by then no one remembered her. One afternoon, while walking, he met an old wrestling friend who mentioned that he owned a private investigation service.

"I've been looking for a woman I knew twenty years ago and almost married," Gene said. "Can you find her?"

His friend put one of his detectives on it, and they quickly found Mary Ann. They left her a decoy message: that a former patient had died and left her some money. Mary Ann couldn't think of a single patient who would have left her money. Intrigued, she called the number.

The detective asked her if she knew Gene.

"Yes, I do," Mary Ann said. "Oh my God! Is he dead?"

"No. He is not. He's very much alive and wants to talk to you."

The very next day, Gene was on a bus to Glen Falls, and Mary Ann was anxiously waiting for him at the nearly empty bus terminal. When she saw him descend the stairs, a cane at his side, she called out, "Gene!"

Gene turned in the direction of her voice. It had been more than twenty years, but they were bridged instantly by that sound. Her voice was the same one he'd fallen in love with in his youth, but it was wiser now, deepened by experience; to him it would always be music.

They didn't speak as they left the station together, holding each other close. They walked slowly, Mary Ann with one arm firmly hugging his waist while he held her hand tightly. Then Gene turned his face into her neck, his breath warm, and began to cry. Mary Ann hugged him harder, with all her strength, grateful tears falling from her own pale gray eyes.

They married three months later, re-creating the world of voice and music they had left behind more than two decades ago.

Big City, Small World

~

JANET WORKED IN the corporate department of a large New York City law firm, and one evening, for the first time in longer than she could remember, she was able to leave her office early. In the elevator, she ran into Gonzalo, another lawyer from her firm, and making small talk, they headed for the subway together.

It was crowded and Janet was tired, so she boarded the first express train, rather than wait for the local, which was more convenient. It happened to be Gonzalo's train as well, so they sat together and continued chatting. She didn't know him well, but they had become acquaintances in the few years she'd been with the firm.

Silently observing them in a seat across the subway car was Keith, a newcomer to the city. He had moved two months ago, having landed a good job in a well-established advertising agency, but he still wasn't comfortable with the grittiness of the Big Apple. Keith had grown up in a small town in Texas and lived in Berkeley, California, while earning his master's degree, and he hadn't known a soul in New York when he'd moved. When he first made his way through Manhattan's concrete-and-steel canyons—passing scores of wandering homeless people, dark patches of seedy streets, and decrepit, almost war-torn buildings—he wondered if he hadn't made a mistake.

Keith caught snippets of the lawyers' conversation, finding himself drawn to Janet. She was of average height, with dark hair, and she had an engaging, open manner that made everything she said seem intriguing.

The train lurched suddenly, and Keith gripped his briefcase in panic. Then, seeing that the other commuters had blithely continued reading the paper or talking, he loosened his grip and tried to relax. He glanced back at Janet and Gonzalo, who were exchanging advice on office politics.

When there was a break in their conversation, Keith leaned forward and asked Janet, "Are you a lawyer?"

Janet noticed him for the first time, taking him in at a glance: He was tall and fair, with two pronounced dimples and large blue eyes, and an easy, unguarded smile.

How incredibly handsome, Janet thought, as she replied, "Yes, I am."

"Where do you work?" Keith said, hoping to strike up a conversation.

Janet replied in a friendly but vague way, "In a big law firm"—not wanting to give away too much personal information to a complete stranger, however good-looking.

Keith immediately picked up on her evasive tone, and he assumed she was giving him the brush-off. Not wanting to seem rude, the gracious Texan nodded and sat back, without saying anything more, and Janet continued her conversation with Gonzalo.

All the way home to her apartment in the East Village, Janet wondered about the attractive stranger on the train. The next day at the office, she sat on her girlfriend's desk.

"Oh, he was so gorgeous!" Janet moaned as she described the tall, blue-eyed man.

"You should have followed him," her friend admonished.

Janet shook her head. "I don't know. You just can't follow some guy. This is New York."

"He was wearing a suit. He had a briefcase. Real scary," her friend responded, sarcastically.

"I know, I know. Now I'm never going to see him again," Janet said, sighing with disappointment.

Janet did not have many more early nights at the office after that. Six months later, wearily making her way to the mailroom in her apartment complex after another twelve-hour day, she picked up her mail and was quickly flipping through it when from behind her a man's voice said, "You look really familiar."

Oh, give me a break, Janet thought, what a tired line. He's going to have to do better than that.

"Did you go to Berkeley?" the man asked.

"No," Janet said, rolling her eyes and turning around, "I didn't go to Berkeley." Then she paused. He *did* look familiar.

"I know," he said. "I met you on the subway."

Suddenly, she remembered too: It was the handsome stranger. They lived in the same building. This time, Keith and Janet introduced themselves and talked for a few minutes, both silently taken aback by the strange coincidence. Keith was just as good-looking as Janet remembered—and now she discovered he was funny and sweet, too—but she was dating someone else at the moment.

Several months passed, and one Sunday night Janet lugged two weeks' worth of dirty clothes up to the fourth floor, but the machines were all in use. "Rats," she muttered. Rather than wait, she decided to try the sixth-floor laundry room, which she almost never used.

She found several free machines and hurriedly threw in her clothes. After adding the detergent, she reached for the bleach and clumsily spilled it all over everything—including the clothes she was wearing and her sterling silver Tiffany key chain, a gift from a client. The bleach turned the silver completely black.

"Oh no!" she cried. "How can I do this?"

Just then, Keith walked into the laundry room. Janet appealed to him, her blue sweatshirt spotted white, "Oh, I'm totally undomesticated! People like me should not be allowed to use bleach. Look at this!" She held up the blackened key chain as final proof of her ineptitude.

"Some silver polish will take care of that," Keith said, unruffled.

"I don't have any silver polish," she lamented.

"I do."

"You do?"

"Yeah. Come over any time. I'm in 5b," he offered graciously.

"Thanks. That's great. I will."

But Janet didn't make it that night. She had plans to go to

dinner and a play with a friend, and when she got back, it was too late. The next several days were the same; she always got home too late to stop by. By Thursday, when Janet still hadn't come over to Keith's apartment as promised, he decided to pay her a visit instead.

That night, heaps of clothes covered the floor of Janet's apartment—she was in the middle of packing for a trip to Los Angeles. In a few days, it would be her thirtieth birthday, and she had planned to celebrate it with some friends on the West Coast. She had just gotten out of the shower and was talking to a friend on the phone when Keith knocked on the door. Janet wondered who it could be. The doorman hadn't announced anyone.

"Who is it?" she called out.

"It's Keith. From upstairs."

"Just a minute!" she yelled, then she whispered to her friend on the phone, "I gotta go. It's the guy from upstairs." She hung up and thought desperately, What am I gonna do? Her apartment was a hopeless mess and she was naked except for a towel. She frantically dashed around gathering her strewn clothes and trying to pile them into some semblance of order— all the while searching for something to wear. Seconds ticked into minutes as she lifted and rejected a dozen items. Finally, after an embarrassingly long time, she gave up and threw on a silk bathrobe. Then she put one hand on the doorknob, slicked back her wet hair with the other, and opened the door.

"Hi," Janet said, flushed and a little out of breath.

"Hi," Keith said. He was holding the silver polish.

"Come in." Janet motioned for him to enter, feeling slightly chagrined. "Sorry about the mess. I'm flying to L.A. tomorrow . . . for my birthday; I'm turning thirty," Janet added.

Keith, meanwhile, was sure Janet's hushed tone and long delay meant that there was another man in the apartment. He exaggerated his nonchalance to hide his suspicion, but Janet brought him the key chain and said, "Here you go."

Unable to extricate himself without seeming rude, Keith sat on a chair and began polishing while they talked. After twenty minutes, however, Keith realized that she wasn't just being polite—anyone hiding in the closet or the bathroom would be stir crazy by now. He and Janet were alone.

Keith began to polish more slowly, dragging out the job, but he needn't have. The more Janet talked to him, the more attracted she became, and the two of them talked until three in the morning.

Finally, Janet looked at the clock and said, "I'm leaving in three hours. I've really got to pack."

"Sure," Keith said, getting up to leave. "When you get back, please call me."

But after she got back, Janet never called. In her mind, she thought, women don't call men, and so she waited for Keith to make the next move. But he never did. She hadn't counted on his gracious Southern manners.

"It's the strangest thing," Janet told a visiting friend a couple weeks later. "I was sure he would call."

"Look," her friend said. "He has really made an effort. He clearly likes you, and he asked you to call him. He's just being polite. I think you should call him."

So she did—and that was all that Keith was waiting for.

After their first date, they saw each other exclusively, and a year and a half later they became engaged. They married in 1994. Today, Janet and Keith live in Manhattan's West Village—and Keith no longer doubts why he moved to the big city.

PART FOUR

The Personals

FOR many people, personal ads are the romance of last resort. We will try just about any dating strategy and idea—go on just about any blind date set up by well-meaning friends—before sitting down to pen a fifteen-word description of ourselves and toss it into the newspaper's personal ad lottery. But it's not always as bad as all that. We find that many people have the same problem: Once we've settled into our jobs and established a circle of friends, meeting a new face can become a rare event. Video dating, personal ads in the newspapers, and now the Internet have become effective ways to meet people. The couples in these stories were also not crazy about the idea of personal ads, but they met through one in a way they had not expected.

Mistaken Identity

~

ELICIA HAD JUST broken up with her boyfriend. Hurt, angry, and not wanting to be alone, she placed a personal ad in the "Singles Wanted" section of a Los Angeles newspaper: "Single female, 23, college graduate, pretty, slim, athletic, good sense of humor looking for guy with same."

After a week, Felicia had received responses from several young men. One day when no one was around, she carefully opened the large envelopes—which were stuffed with photographs and notes from the men, ages twenty-two to thirty—and studied their profiles with all the delight of a teenager on an extravagant shopping spree. Hmm. This one looks kind of cute, she thought of a young prospect, Steve. He had wavy, blond hair and blue eyes. In the picture, he stood casually next to a girl he said was his sister.

Later that morning, Felicia left a message for Steve and went out to do some errands. In the afternoon, Steve's roommate, whose name was also Steve, came home and listened to the messages on the machine.

"Hi. I'm calling for Steve. I'm Felicia, the girl who placed the ad—" Steve didn't recognize the name and didn't know anything about an ad. Wrong number, he thought. Automatically, he erased the message and went on to the next one.

Felicia didn't think anything of it when Steve did not return her call, and after a couple of months, she had gotten back together with her old boyfriend. One afternoon she handed her friend Robin a bulging manila envelope.

"I won't be needing these anymore," Felicia said. "Maybe you'd like to look through them."

"What's this?" Robin asked.

She dumped the contents of the envelope onto the sofa and flipped through a couple of photographs.

"Hey, " Robin said. "No way! I can't believe you actually did this."

Felicia merely shrugged. Robin ran her hands through the pile. "I feel like a kid in a candy shop."

Robin would never have put a personal ad in a newspaper. She was outgoing and attractive—and never had to worry about getting dates. She had recently graduated from San Diego State University and was now living in Los Angeles with her mother. She wasn't sure what she wanted to do next with her life, but she had some strange feeling that she should be in L.A., even though she missed San Diego and wanted to move back. She was not usually so indecisive. As she sifted through the stack of letters and photos, Robin thought to herself, What do I have to lose? She had no serious boyfriend at the time.

"Have fun," Felicia said, swinging her bag over her shoulder and heading to her boyfriend's place.

Alone at home that evening, Robin paged through the stack of profiles until one captured her attention—it was Steve, the same one who had caught Felicia's eye. Robin picked up the phone, hesitated, then dialed the number.

That evening, the other Steve—the one who had erased Felicia's message—was at home arguing with his brother, who was visiting from Wisconsin. Steve was itching to go out on the town, but his brother just wanted to stay in.

"Hey, what's the point of coming all the way from Wisconsin if you just want to sit inside?" Steve didn't bother waiting for an answer. "Fine, you stay here. I'm going out."

He grabbed his jacket and headed toward the door. Just then, the phone rang.

"Hi, is Steve in?" a pretty female voice asked.

"Yeah, this is Steve," he said, not recognizing the woman.

"This may sound kind of strange to you," Robin said. "You don't really know me. But my roommate put an ad in a personal section and she gave me the responses that she got to her ad. Anyway, she got back together with her boyfriend and told me I could look through the stuff she got."

"Uh-huh," Steve said, intrigued.

"Well, anyway, you responded. I was looking at your picture and read your note, so I thought I'd call you myself."

"I see," Steve said, playing along, thinking she sounded attractive. "Well, I'm glad you called."

They made some small talk, and Steve started to warm to his role. Then he mentioned that his brother was visiting from Wisconsin.

"Oh, so you have a brother *and* a sister?"

"Well—"

"You sent a picture of yourself with your sister."

"Oh, I guess I did."

"Does your brother live in Wisconsin?"

"Yeah . . ." Steve stalled, gauging the best way to answer what had become a trick question, "he does."

"I thought you mentioned your family was from California?"

Steve could see that he was boxing himself into a corner and that he'd better come clean before it went much further.

"Robin, I'm not the Steve who responded to your ad."

"You're not Steve?" she asked incredulously.

"No, I mean, my name *is* Steve. I had a roommate also named Steve. He must have been the one who responded to your ad."

"You mean my roommate's ad," Robin corrected.

"Right . . . her ad. Anyway, he moved out a couple of months ago."

Robin realized she knew nothing about the person she was talking to—or what he looked like. "This is kind of strange," she said. "Maybe I should call the other Steve, since he answered the ad."

"Well, don't bother about Steve. He's moving to Washington. Besides—" Steve suddenly felt like he didn't want the call to end. "I'm much better looking." Steve's brother rolled his eyes. "I think you should go out with me anyway."

They talked some more, and after a few minutes Robin decided to go for it. They set a date a few days later to meet at a restaurant.

On the appointed day, Steve showed up early. He wanted to be prepared. That's when he realized he had no idea what she looked like, and there is no dearth of beautiful women in L.A. Just then a leggy brunette walked toward him.

"Oh, she's coming my way. I hope that's her. God, she's gorgeous."

The woman breezed right by. Anxiety set in. He looked around nervously. The restaurant was practically empty. Another pretty girl walked toward him. She wore a white cotton shirt and blue jeans. She had bright blue eyes, freckles, and thick, brown hair. It was Robin, and she smiled warmly at him, relieved that she found him attractive.

"Steve?" she asked, with a tinge of nervousness in her voice.

"Yes. I'm Steve," he said, rising to greet her, his spirits high. He couldn't have been happier—she had a natural look, like the girls he knew in Wisconsin.

Over dinner, they fell into a lengthy conversation. Steve had graduated from the University of Wisconsin, and he had moved to Los Angeles to break into the entertainment business. He'd gotten a job in the mailroom of an entertainment company and was currently working his way up from the bottom.

Before long, Robin and Steve were talking as if they were old friends, and they stayed out until two in the morning. As they sat in a quiet pub, Steve took Robin's hand and kissed her affectionately. He had never done that on a first date before, but with Robin it seemed natural.

THE NEXT day Steve flew to Cleveland: He was the best man at a good friend's wedding. At one point Steve surprised himself when he admitted to his friend, "I think I met my wife last night." Steve had dated a woman for four years, and they never came close to discussing the subject of marriage, and now he was bringing it up after one date. On his return to L.A., he and Robin saw each other all the time.

After they'd been dating for a month, Steve was with some friends at a restaurant when his old roommate—the original Steve—walked in. He had heard about what had happened.

"Hey, you stole my date!" he said, practically shouting.

"She wasn't your date," Steve shot back. "She didn't even place the ad." The other Steve was a little upset at what seemed like trickery on his roommate's part, and it took him a while to calm down.

"Okay, can I at least get a finder's fee?" he said, managing to laugh.

And as if these series of coincidences weren't enough, this case of mistaken identity later achieved a small measure of notoriety. At a small gathering of women, Robin's mother approached a friend who was talking to a third woman, a stranger. They all chatted together for a bit when the third woman said, "You're not going to believe this, but my son's roommate stole my son's date."

"What do you mean?" the mutual friend asked.

"My son responded to a personal ad in the paper. The woman who placed the ad called and my son was out at the time . . ."

Robin's mom suddenly realized what they were talking about. She quickly interrupted, "Hey, that's my daughter you're talking about! She didn't place the ad!" Then she told them the rest of the unusual story.

From their first meeting, Robin and Steve knew they were meant to be together. Just three months later, they were engaged. They married in 1994 and now live in Milwaukee with their daughter. Steve works for the family business.

Red Hair

⌒

THE RURAL TOWN in southern Utah where John grew up was so small it did not have a traffic light. In John's hometown, people generally married straight out of high school and wasted no time starting their families. Of the twenty-four graduates in his high school class, John was one of three who went on to college. By age thirty, John continued to be a local anomaly, not so much because he was one of the few Catholics in a predominantly Mormon town, but because he was still single.

After graduating from the University of Southern Utah, where he had majored in journalism and political science, John settled in the small town of Richfield, where he took a job as a state welfare case worker in a functional, nondescript government office. There wasn't a lot to do where he lived—there wasn't even a movie theater—and except for an occasional night out in a local bar, John preferred to stay at home in the evenings and read a good book.

As the years passed, John became friends with another case worker, Debbie, who shared his office. Debbie was smart and spunky and also single. They would confide in each other, talking often about their desire to get married and their struggles to find someone. During a lull in a long afternoon, John confessed his vision of the perfect mate.

"She has to be smart," John said. "That's a must. Funny would be good, too."

"And tall," Debbie threw in. John was six-foot-five.

"And red hair," John added, smiling sheepishly. "I just have a thing about a woman with red hair."

But there was no one to date in Richfield. The months wore on, and John was unable to escape the monotony as one could not escape the summer heat. He was tired of being single. On the rare occasion when John did have a date, he usually found that he and the woman had little in common. Once, he and a date were watching the news after dinner, and the news anchor mentioned it was the anniversary of Robert Kennedy's death. "Who's that?" his date asked. John just shook his head and suggested that they call it a night.

One afternoon, Debbie was looking through the personal section in the *Salt Lake City Tribune*.

"Hey, John," she said, "I've got an idea. Why don't we put personal ads in the paper?"

"What?" He looked up from the open case file on his desk. "A lonely hearts ad? No way. That's not me."

But Debbie persisted. "Come on, these are just great. Listen to this: 'Handsome, tall male, nonsmoker, loves hiking, skiing, romantic restaurants, financially stable—'"

"Spare me. Everyone says that. Wait till you meet him: short, broke, skied only once and had to be brought down by the ski instructor on a gurney."

"Okay. Okay. Let's put one in—just for fun. It's totally anonymous, and free. Let's just see what happens. You don't have to answer any of them."

"I don't know . . ."

"We'll be totally honest. We'll describe ourselves perfectly, no fluff."

As a lark, John agreed, and they each placed a personal ad. John's read:

Teddy Bear, 6'5", looks like John Goodman. I'm academic and like jazz and blues, looking for someone intelligent with good sense of humor.

They decided to run their ads twice a week for a few months. While Debbie waited anxiously for responses, John nearly forgot about his until the letters and voicemail messages started pouring in. During breaks at work, they read the letters together and listened to the voicemail messages on speakerphone—shaking their heads, rolling their eyes, and cracking jokes. It became a great way to break up the monotony of the day.

After reading one letter, Debbie exclaimed, "A golf pro? Could you see me with a golf pro?"

John read a letter from a woman who was in the army.

"There aren't enough men in the army?" Debbie cracked.

"She says she doesn't want to marry a general!"

Then, assuming a stern falsetto, John mimicked, 'I am in the army. This is what I do. Don't try to change it. This is the way it is.' Yes, Ma'am!" John stood at attention, saluted, and tossed the letter down.

"So when are you calling her?" Debbie asked, laughing.

But after three months, the fun began to fade. The joke became a little tired; the truth was, they hadn't found anyone who seemed even remotely interesting among the dozens and dozens of responses. John never answered a single ad.

"Maybe we should change the ad this time," Debbie suggested one afternoon.

"I've had enough," John said. "Game's over."

"Oh come on, John, just one more time. I promise, this will be the last time."

"The last time," he said.

One afternoon, a couple of weeks later, Debbie closed the office door, dialed the personal ad phone mail number, and pressed the speaker button. As always, she grabbed a pen just in case. Distracted, John jotted some notes on a new case file, not really listening.

"I'm five-eleven, twenty-eight," a soft, female voice said.

"John," Debbie whispered significantly, "five feet eleven!"

"I also love jazz and blues—" John turned toward the speakerphone. "I have a master's degree in nursing. I'm Irish Catholic—" Debbie looked at John, opening her eyes wide. With a touch of coyness, the woman mentioned she thought John Goodman was pretty cute. Then she added at the end, "Oh yes, I have red hair."

Debbie's jaw dropped, and there was complete silence in the room. For the first time since they'd begun listening to the messages, neither of them cracked a joke.

Debbie replayed Colleen's message, wrote down her phone number, and placed it on John's desk.

"You have to call her," Debbie said.

"But the ad was just a prank," John said unconvincingly.

"You can't let this one go," Debbie insisted.

John knew she was right. In his heart, he knew he would always regret it if he didn't at least call.

That night, John dialed the number. He was nervous at first, but Colleen was intelligent and a good conversationalist, and she quickly put him at ease. They joked about their common oddity: their single status. An unmarried, twenty-eight-year-old nurse in Salt Lake City was a rare find. They spoke for more than an hour, and over the next few weeks, they had several long conversations, feeling a growing rapport. Eventually, they were calling each other every single day.

After a month and a half of telephone conversations, they decided to meet; John would drive up to Salt Lake City. On the day of his trip, a nasty snowstorm choked the roads. About halfway up, John hit a roadblock and could not go any farther. The depth of his disappointment surprised him. He turned back and found a place to call Colleen.

"I'm sorry, Colleen, but the roads headed north are blocked. I can't get through." John apologized over and over, finally ending with, "I'll call you when I get home."

The next day, John sent Colleen a bouquet of flowers—Colleen told him later that it was the first time anyone had ever sent her flowers.

Finally, in November, they met for the first time in the parking lot of a home-improvement store in Salt Lake City. As Colleen approached his car, John saw that she was very tall, big-boned, and had gorgeous red hair. He got out and politely shook her hand.

They went to the annual Festival of Trees: a celebration of the most beautiful and elaborate Christmas tree decorations. Then on their way to dinner, they passed Salt Lake City's only Catholic cathedral.

"That's such a beautiful church," Colleen said. "I'd like to get married there someday."

After that first day, John knew she was the one he was going to marry—and they did in 1995, at the church they had passed on their first date.

PART FIVE

Bad Things Happen to Good People

ONE *of the tenets of many spiritual disciplines is that our lives have purpose, and that every place we go, every person we meet, every event is meaningful. This is easy to believe when things go well or turn out like we expect, but sometimes a terrible tragedy or event will shake our faith. What is the point of our pain? we feel; what possible purpose could it serve? Ultimately, as creatures of the physical world experiencing time and space through only our five senses, our knowledge of a higher reality is limited. Without the full spiritual picture, we cannot know all the reasons for things that occur in our lives, but every once in a while the meaning behind a painful event becomes clear. Perhaps we find ourselves unexpectedly changed in a positive way or led to a new situation or person we wouldn't have met otherwise. In these stories, difficult circumstances are what lead two people to find each other.*

The Layover

⁓

D R. ABRAHAM TWERSKI is a renowned psychiatrist and rabbi who descends from a long line of revered Chassidic leaders. The Chassidim are a branch of Orthodox Judaism; their worship of God emphasizes joy and emotion with dance and song.

Dr. Twerski founded and operates a successful drug rehabilitation center in Pittsburgh and has authored several popular books on drug addiction and spiritual well-being. On the Sabbath and holidays, he retreats to his home, where he invites guests to share festive meals with his family. At these meals, he relates remarkable Chassidic tales that have been handed down from generation to generation—legacies of the Jewish oral tradition.

During one Sabbath meal, after Dr. Twerski had related a particularly striking tale, one of the guests politely suggested, "Why don't you collect these stories in a book? They're so moving, but I can barely remember enough details to do them any justice when I try to relate them."

Dr. Twerski was silent and looked thoughtfully at the man.

"I used to say the same thing to my uncle," he said after a few moments.

Later that year, Dr. Twerski published his first work of nonfiction stories, titled *From Generation to Generation*.

IN VENICE, California, Marilyn received a copy of Dr. Twerski's new book from a friend as a thank-you gift. In her thirties, Marilyn was divorced and raising her young son, David. She had not grown up in a religious household, and she knew little about Judaism, her religion. At the recommendation of a friend, she attended a few lectures on it, and she was so moved that she began to go to synagogue and learn more. Soon, she was incorporating some of the practices of Orthodox Judaism into her life, such as keeping kosher and observing the Sabbath.

Marilyn was a respected lecturer in sports nutrition, and she had been on the staff of the 1984 Summer Olympics. In June 1986, she had a speaking engagement in Atlantic City, and everything went smoothly until her return flight home.

On her itinerary, she had one layover in Philadelphia, then a second short one in Pittsburgh, where she would board a final plane to Los Angeles. The flight from Atlantic City to Philadelphia went without a hitch, and she was eager and excited to return home and see her son, David, who would be leaving for his first trip to sleep-away camp that coming weekend. She sighed. It would be the first time they would be apart for an extended period, and she couldn't help feeling a little wistful about it. I guess my little boy is growing up, she thought.

But as she exited the gate at the Philadelphia airport, she heard over the loudspeaker: "Flight 181 to Pittsburgh will be delayed fifteen minutes because of weather conditions. We apologize for any inconvenience."

"Oh no," Marilyn said under her breath. She felt a flutter of panic and checked her watch: Luckily, she still would have just enough time to make her connecting flight to Los Angeles.

As she waited impatiently, however, there was another announcement: "Flight 181 to Pittsburgh will be delayed another twenty minutes."

"Don't they know people have connecting planes to catch!" she cried.

Her chest tightened. Now she really feared she would miss her connecting flight, and she ran to the reservations desk to see about other planes to L.A. But she soon discovered there were none that could solve her particular dilemma: As an observant Jew, she could not drive or take an airplane on a Jewish holiday or the Sabbath; Jewish law forbade it. A two-day Jewish holiday was to begin after sundown that evening, which was a Wednesday, followed immediately by the Sabbath, which would not end until late Saturday night. If she missed her flight, there was no way she could get home before Sunday afternoon. And her son was leaving for camp Sunday morning!

Everything was falling apart. She still had to help David pack—and how would she get him to the airport on Sunday? Even if he got a ride from a friend, how could she miss sending him off on his first long trip away from home? And where would she stay for the next three days—so she could properly observe the holiday and Sabbath? These thoughts played over and over in her head until they finally announced that flight 181 was ready for boarding.

She fretted the entire way from Philadelphia to Pittsburgh,

hoping and praying that she would make it. As the plane landed and arrived at the terminal, she grabbed her duffel bag and dashed to the exit, slightly crazed. She ran all the way to the connecting gate, but it was no use: The flight to Los Angeles had already left.

"Oh no!" she cried aloud, suddenly paralyzed by her anger and frustration. For a moment she just stood there and sobbed, feeling the sting of life's unfairness.

After a few minutes, she'd calmed down and gathered her wits about her. She called her rabbi in Los Angeles.

"Stay in Pittsburgh for the holiday and the Sabbath," he advised her. "We'll help you with your son. Find a Jewish family to stay with."

Since she didn't know anyone in Pittsburgh, she tried to reach some local synagogues. But with the holiday approaching, their offices were closed. She tried a few other Jewish organizations. No luck. Panic began to overtake her again. She checked her wallet; she had almost no money. She had never felt so helpless.

Then, suddenly, the name Abraham Twerski popped into her head. He lived in Pittsburgh. Yes. Yes, she was sure of it. She remembered his name from inside the jacket cover of his book, *From Generation to Generation*. He runs a hospital for drug addicts in Pittsburgh! I must find him!

She took a cab to Twerski's hospital, spending nearly all the cash she had. She bolted inside and found Dr. Twerski's office, but it was empty. She uttered another cry of despair.

Marilyn found one of the doctor's associates. "Please give me his number at home," she asked.

"I'm sorry. I can't do that," the associate replied. Marilyn explained her situation, but her frenetic, panicked manner only made the associate more nervous.

"Of all people, the rabbi would understand," Marilyn pleaded. "Please, you have to help me. I don't even have any money left for a cab."

Marilyn's distress was so genuine that the associate finally said that she would call Dr. Twerski's son, who also worked at the hospital. She called him at home, and he arranged for Marilyn to spend the holiday and Sabbath with a family near the Twerski residence. Dr. Twerski's son arrived at the hospital twenty minutes later and drove Marilyn to the neighbor's house. She almost couldn't contain her gratitude and relief.

As he dropped her off, he wished her a happy holiday.

"And you too, happy holiday," she replied. "And thank you again!"

Marilyn's hostess greeted her warmly at the door, surrounded by the exquisite aroma of freshly baked bread. "We're delighted to have you," she said. "Come, let me show you to your room." She led Marilyn upstairs and left her alone.

Relieved but still worried about her son, Marilyn immediately called a good friend in Venice to make sure he would be taken care of and would get to the airport all right. Then she called David and explained what had happened. She concealed her own disappointment, reassuring herself that he was in good hands.

Then Marilyn lay back on the bed, exhausted and hungry, and began to relax for the first time in hours. She replayed the day's tiring events in her head. She freshened up and went downstairs. The house was full of holiday spirit, and the good cheer and smells of cooking were intoxicating. She lit candles with the other women in the dining room as they waited for the men to return from prayer at the synagogue.

The men arrived with great noise and abundant greetings, and the family sat Marilyn at a place of honor for the evening meal. The warmth and the joyous songs uplifted and enraptured Marilyn in a way she hadn't expected—creating a sense of openness inside her to whatever destiny had to offer. When she went to bed that night, she fell into a deep and peaceful sleep.

The next day, it was arranged that Marilyn would have lunch at the Twerskis' home nearby. After hearing of Marilyn's mishaps, Mrs. Twerski said, "There must be a reason for all this."

At lunch, Marilyn felt the magic of the previous night lingering inside her. Across the table, several men were engaged in various conversations, and one of them, Steven, began to catch her attention. He had light, kind eyes and a warm manner, and he displayed an admirable conviction in his beliefs. He was also quite funny. Every so often Marilyn laughed at one of his offhanded comments, and as the meal progressed, it seemed his lighthearted jokes were meant especially for her.

At the end of the meal, Steven offered to walk Marilyn home. They walked slowly, talking easily and comfortably. It was not long before Marilyn felt as though she had known him all her life. She was disappointed when they arrived at the house where she was staying, hoping for any excuse to continue talking. For the rest of the day, all she could think about was Steven.

The next morning, over coffee, she asked her hostess where Steven would be having lunch after the morning synagogue service; Marilyn arranged to eat lunch in the same place. But when lunchtime came, Steven didn't appear. When Marilyn made some casual inquiries about him, she found out he was dating someone. Oh, how could I have been so wrong? Marilyn thought. Was I the only one feeling a connection? She thought that perhaps the wine and song from the night before had deluded her, and she couldn't help feeling disappointed.

On Saturday night, Marilyn quietly packed her few things for her trip back home the next morning. The telephone rang. It was Steven.

"Hi. I so enjoyed talking to you," he said.

Marilyn's heart skipped a beat. "Me, too."

"I changed my lunch plans and came over the next day to where you're staying so we could have lunch together. But I guess you went somewhere else." Marilyn smiled, but decided not to say anything. "Are you leaving tomorrow?" he asked.

"Yes. First thing in the morning."

"Would you like to go out for a drink tonight?"

"Yes," Marilyn answered, "I would."

That night they went out, and their connection felt just as strong as it had at lunch two days before. And as it turned out, he wasn't dating anyone seriously. The next day he drove her to the airport.

When Marilyn got home, she was just pulling her key out of the latch when the telephone rang. It was Steven.

"Was your trip alright?" he asked.

"Yes. I just walked in."

Then he dispensed with further small talk. "I'd like to come to L.A. to see you."

The next week, Steven went to L.A., and not long afterward, Marilyn visited him in Pittsburgh. Five weeks later, neither of them had doubts about their feelings for each other, and they became engaged. After they married, they settled in Pittsburgh not far from the Twerskis, and they had four more children together.

But their fated match was set in motion long before fog delayed Marilyn's flight. Who was the young gentleman who politely suggested that Dr. Twerski memorialize his Chassidic tales in a book? That gentleman was Steven.

Love on Two Wheels

PAUL SEETHED WITH anger as he sat, stuck in his car, in heavy freeway traffic. It was a typical Friday afternoon on a California highway, but in Paul's mind he shouldn't have been on the road at all. He was heading forty-five minutes north to pick up his friend Corey, so they could then turn right around and head south to San Diego, where they had to catch a bus to Mexico in a few hours.

This is insane! Paul thought, as he punched the steering wheel. I'm such a jerk to let him convince me to drive up here—Corey should be the one picking *me* up.

The next day Paul and Corey were to join ten thousand other Southern Californians in an annual fifty-mile bike race along some of the Pacific's most gorgeous coastline in Baja California, just south of the Mexican border. This would be Paul's sixth straight year in the race, and mounted on a bike rack on top of his car was his brand-new ten-speed, racing bike—the latest addition to his expensive collection. The car moved forward in a jerking motion as Paul pressed and released the brakes in the stop-and-go traffic, and the smog was beginning to burn his eyes. At this rate, they'd never catch the bus in San Diego.

The usually mild-mannered and easygoing Paul was angrier than he could ever remember. The only reason he was making this time-consuming detour was because Corey had just bought a new luxury car, and he had refused to carry the bikes, fearing they would scratch his shiny new paint.

By the time Paul finally reached his freeway exit, he was fuming, and he raced toward Corey's apartment. He made a sharp right into Corey's garage—and heard a sickening crunch of metal. He instantly slammed on the brakes, but it was too late. He sat in his car for a second, his blood boiling, and then got out to survey the damage: His new bike—strapped to the roof—had slammed into the garage's door frame. It was totaled, the once-sleek steel now a crumpled mess.

Paul knocked on Corey's door, and when his friend answered, he told him, "I'm not going."

Paul explained what had happened, and Corey sucked in his breath and shook his head.

"You're a prima donna for not wanting to use your car," Paul said, letting loose some of his pent-up anger. "I just don't want to go now."

Corey tried to calm him down. "Come on. We've got this whole trip planned. There's no point in not going. We'll just stop at your place and get one of your other bikes."

"I just bought this bike," Paul replied in a sharp tone, implying that Corey was missing the point. But Paul had ridden in the race the last five years, and Corey, knowing Paul would regret missing the race, tried to appeal to his rational side.

"Look, there are going to be ten thousand people in that race—half of them female. That makes about five thousand women."

Eventually, Paul, who had ended a five-year relationship three months earlier, agreed, but he refused to shake his foul mood.

They got on the freeway again, but traffic was just as bad headed south, and they soon could do no more than inch forward.

"Look at this traffic," Paul complained. "We'll never make it in time to catch the bus."

"We'll make it," Corey assured him.

"Let's just turn around," Paul said every five miles or so.

"We'll make it. Stop worrying," Corey replied each time.

"Damn it. I'm not going to be able to ride my new bike." Paul turned to Corey. "I mean it, let's just turn around."

"We're going to pick up another bike," Corey insisted, summoning a patience he didn't know he had.

And indeed, they eventually got to Paul's place and picked up his mountain bike—it was much slower than the new bike, but it would have to do. From there, the thirty-three-year-old men—Paul a stockbroker and Corey a market researcher—who had traded in white starched shirts and ties for t-shirts and cycling shorts, caught the bus just in time.

On the bus, a party atmosphere soon broke loose among the dozen or so cyclists also aboard, and Paul was not completely immune. Once they had arrived in the town where the race would start, and Paul and Corey had finished a succulent lobster dinner and several *cervezas* in a restaurant crowded with tomorrow's racers, Paul was close to feeling pretty good.

The next morning, Paul and Corey sat perched on their bikes at the starting line, waiting with thousands of other riders for the race to begin. To their right, the vast and commanding ocean created a perfect setting for an already pristine late spring day.

The bikers crawled along for the first mile or so, until gradually they began breaking away from each other and hitting their stride. Paul could not keep up with Corey, who was on his racing bike, and after five miles, Paul lost sight of his friend. For a while Paul rode alone, enjoying the crisp air and the sight of the jagged mountains as they rose from Mexico's wild beaches.

Up ahead, Paul spotted a pair of shapely calves powering a bicycle, and he rode silently behind, admiring them. He had a soft spot for calves, beautifully shaped and flung casually one over the other, peering shyly beneath a skirt, or, as in this case, firm and lovely and pedaling a bicycle. Emboldened, he rode up alongside the woman to whom the perfect calves belonged. She wore a streamlined bike helmet and dark sport sunglasses. A few loose hairs whipped about her helmet, but Paul could not see her face—she looked like a giant bug. He flashed her a smile, and since she seemed to be bopping up and down as if to music, he said to her, "What tune do you have in your head?"

"How did you know?" she asked, surprised.

They struck up a conversation as they rode. Her name was Tammy. After they discovered they both spoke French, Paul began, with much flourish, wooing her in that language of love. At the rest stops, however, they separated as they replenished themselves for more riding. Paul kept an eye on her from a short distance, starting up when she did. He couldn't tell for sure if she was waiting for him also, but he made sure they rode the rest of the race together.

At the finish line, Tammy removed her helmet and sunglasses. Paul almost hesitated to look—but as he did he thought, "She's gorgeous. What luck! Charming, smart, *and* beautiful." He had sense enough to realize that his good luck extended to yesterday's fiasco. If he had ridden his faster racing bike, he probably would have missed her altogether.

After that, Tammy and Paul took many more rides together. He knew several months after meeting Tammy at the road race that he wanted to marry her. Paul and Tammy married in 1994. Today, they are raising their family in the wide-open spaces of Orcas Island, Washington.

Driving Sheila

⌒

ON AN OTHERWISE postcard-perfect day in November 1993, an out-of-control fire tore through the hills of Malibu, California, indiscriminately scorching sagebrush, chaparral, and dozens of homes that dotted the landscape.

Smoke billowed in great columns, choking the sky, and firefighters signaled homeowners to evacuate. Sheila had lived in Malibu for ten years, but now she had only a few moments to run through her house and decide what to keep. Because the trunk of her car was filled with camping equipment, she could only take what she could stuff into her back seat. Sheila rushed back and forth from room to room, stalled with indecision, until she uttered a cry of despair. Frantic, she grabbed her computer, her clients' files, and an antique letter opener—a present from her mother from years before. Then she drove down the winding road to safety.

Trembling, she parked her car and watched as fire rose over the ridge, engulfing the hillside and all her possessions. At thirty-nine, she had lost everything.

Sheila slowly put her life back together. She moved into a

one-bedroom apartment in Pacific Palisades, a well-to-do community that rests on the bluffs overlooking the Pacific Ocean. An accountant, Sheila had worked at home before the fire, but her new place was too small. When a friend offered her the use of an office in Westlake, she accepted, despite the forty-five-minute commute.

It seemed like the worst was over. With surprising speed, Sheila accumulated new possessions and adjusted to her new routine. Then, in June 1995, she became mysteriously ill. Doctors could not diagnose her ailment, which grew more serious by the day. Fearing for her life, doctors admitted Sheila into the hospital and began treating her with massive doses of antibiotics as unidentified infections raged inside her. After a week, she had stabilized, though she still felt sick and listless. There was nothing more the doctors could do for her, however, so they released her from the hospital and she went home.

Petite, with lovely pale skin and brown hair, Sheila was determined not to let her inexplicable illness destroy her life. Still too weak to make the drive to work, she called a car service she had used when she lived in Malibu.

When Eliot, the owner of the company, overheard his clerk scheduling a pickup for "Sheila Gunther," he immediately asked to take the call.

"Sheila," Eliot said enthusiastically, "it's been such a long time."

Eliot had not heard from Sheila for several years before the fire, though she had used his car service from time to time for ten years before that. Eliot had an easygoing, joking manner, and they soon became friends over the phone. After a while, whenever Sheila called the company, she always asked to speak to Eliot, since their conversations were so spirited and convivial. Once, when Sheila had visited the office to collect some receipts for a tax audit, Eliot caught his first glimpse of her from a distance. But Sheila, who was engaged at the time, was too busy looking through papers to notice anyone admiring her.

After a brief but warm conversation in which the two friends caught up, Eliot made arrangements for a driver to pick her up the next morning.

But the next day, when she got a call from the driver telling her that he was waiting in the alley outside, Sheila thought she recognized a familiar voice. She peered out the window and saw a large, black Mercedes—not the company's trademark van. Eliot? she wondered.

Sheila grabbed her things and hobbled slowly down the stairs. Eliot immediately leaped up to help her.

A little surprised and taken aback that Eliot himself had come to pick her up, Sheila asked, half laughing, "Have you changed your cars?"

"No, I didn't have any other available drivers," Eliot said, shrugging nonchalantly.

For the first time they had more than a few minutes to talk, and they spent the entire forty-five-minute drive to Westlake getting to know each other better than they had during the ten years of their acquaintance. As usual, Eliot's quick wit sparked the conversation and put Sheila at ease, and she shared with him some of her recent troubles.

At the end of the day, Eliot was waiting outside her office, again to Sheila's surprise, and that week Eliot drove her several more times to and from work. Each time, his charm and good humor lifted her spirits.

After two weeks off antibiotics, Sheila took a turn for the worse. Despite repeated visits, her doctors were still unable to treat her mysterious infection. She became too sick to go to work, and one day she was so weak she could hardly get out of bed. Sheila's sister often came over to help, but Sheila realized she needed full-time care. She called her parents, who agreed to come and stay with her for three weeks. When they arrived at the airport, Eliot's car service was there to pick them up.

One day in the middle of her parents' stay, Sheila got a call from Eliot.

She was confused. "Oh, I didn't book a ride."

"I know," Eliot said. "I just called to see how you were doing."

"I'm feeling a bit better." Sheila was touched by his concern, and they spoke for a few minutes. Sheila *was* feeling somewhat better, and she hoped to return to work soon, but there was no way to know just how long it would take.

After a couple more weeks, Eliot couldn't wait anymore. One afternoon he called Sheila and asked her out on a date. Sheila was surprised to get his call.

"Eliot," Sheila said, affecting a light tone, "I can barely walk."

"Don't worry, we'll work it out," he said.

They decided to go to dinner and a movie. After the meal, Eliot helped Sheila into the car and they headed for the theater. But at the first stoplight, he turned to her, leaned over, and kissed her. Then he looked deeply into her face with his gentle, brown eyes that drew her toward him. "We are going to know each other a very long time," Eliot told her. Sheila didn't know how to respond; she had once been engaged to a man she had dated for eight years, but it had broken off badly. As they drove on, Eliot took her hand, and waves of calming energy soothed her.

At forty-nine, Eliot was practically a confirmed bachelor. He was successful and adventurous, a tai chi aficionado, and he had been in several long relationships. When friends would ask him why none of these relationships ever ended in marriage, he typically answered, "I never met the right one."

They saw each other several more times over the next few weeks. When Sheila decided to take a short trip to Chicago to visit her family, Eliot naturally drove her to the airport. They hugged and kissed good-bye, and then Eliot said, softly but with certainty, "I'm going to marry you one day."

The next few months would prove to be the most difficult of Sheila's life. After her brief recovery, her health again worsened and the doctors decided she needed surgery. Although they were still little more than friends, it seemed only natural that Eliot stayed with her during the operation and returned with her when she went home—where she lay unconscious for three days—to tend to her as she recovered.

Over the next several weeks, Eliot took care of Sheila. As he sat by her bedside, he would sometimes kiss her, but nothing more. Sheila did not have the energy; her illness left her drained and exhausted. In quiet moments alone, she would become depressed and wonder why Eliot ever chose to stay with her. She felt unattractive and despaired of ever recovering. She couldn't believe him when he stroked her face and told her she was beautiful.

A month later, Sheila underwent a second painful surgery, and Eliot remained devoted and steadfast.

A month after that, in early 1996, Sheila faced the prospect of a third surgery, but another doctor, a specialist, finally agreed to see her. He treated her with an obscure remedy usually reserved for heart patients, and it seemed to work. At last, she was on the road to permanent recovery.

Sheila couldn't contain her joy at finally having her life back, and most amazing of all, she had found Eliot. It seemed like all the terrible traumas of the last two and a half years had led her to this man, who had stayed with her and loved her through her darkest hours. Their romance flourished, and in a year they became engaged. They wed in the summer of 1998—Eliot's first marriage at the age of fifty-one.

One afternoon, Eliot asked Sheila, "Remember the first time I picked you up?"

"Yes. You said there were no other drivers."

Eliot couldn't contain his smile. "Well, that wasn't true."

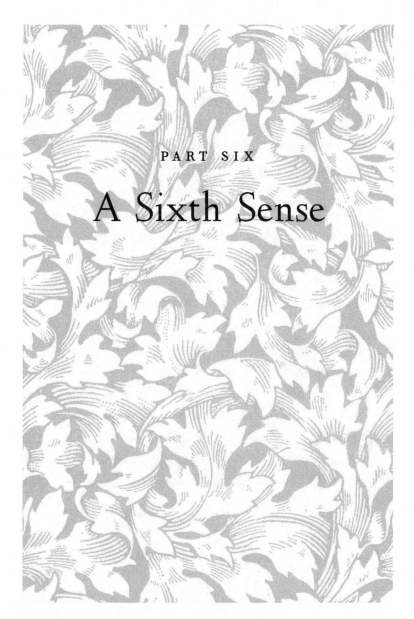

PART SIX

A Sixth Sense

IT *happens more often than we realize: Two people meet and know instantly that they will marry. We have all sorts of phrases to describe this phenomenon—love at first sight, chemistry, struck by cupid's arrow—but what exactly is this inexplicable, sometimes instantaneous connection some people experience? The feeling is more than just physical attraction or infatuation; it's a deep knowing, as if our souls themselves are guiding us.*

Some people call it a sixth sense, an extrasensory perception of reality that we all have access to. Most of us may experience it only once or twice, though that single occasion can also transform our lives. If we believe in the existence of radio waves, it's not hard to believe that there exist other invisible ways to communicate, or a psychic sense. Sometimes it's just a strong intuition or an inexplicable feeling of well-being around another person, but in the following stories, a spiritual or psychic connection is the silent force guiding two people together.

A Debate with God

$\sim$

$\mathcal{A}$T THIRTY-FOUR, Lyn was making more money than she had ever dreamed. She wore stylish suits with short skirts and the latest Italian, high-heeled pumps, and drove around Los Angeles in a shiny, red sports car with her three-hundred-dollar cell phone pasted to her ear.

One day after her lunchtime workout, she returned to the office.

"Hi, Sal," Lyn said to her secretary. "Any messages?"

"A couple of insurance adjusters. The Normans called. They want to settle their case. And a Mike Glazer—"

"Mike Glazer?" Lyn interrupted. "Oh, the lawyer with the Delorean. Why are the only guys I date lawyers with Deloreans?"

"Maybe because *you're* a lawyer?"

"Throw it away," Lyn said, waiving her hand at the offending message slip. She'd had enough of blow-dried men with plastic personalities and spaceships for cars.

She went to her office, swiveled 'round in her chair, and called her real estate agent.

"How's escrow going?" Lyn asked her. "Will it close on the tenth?"

After a brief update, Lyn hung up and sat back in her chair. She wasn't going to wait around for the perfect man to appear and transform her life, so she'd done the only sensible thing: bought a couple of dogs and made an offer to buy a house on her own.

The next week, her friend Peggy called to invite her to dinner. Peggy and her husband were ex-hippies, spiritually minded, and incredibly generous with what little they had. Lyn liked being around them.

"I want you to meet someone at dinner next week," Peggy told her. "His name is Morty."

"Sure, I'm willing to meet just about anyone," Lyn replied.

But Morty was not much to look at: He was short, slovenly, and his ripped T-shirt peered from beneath a sorry-looking jacket, which, if it were a building, would have been condemned. He was forty-two, unmarried, and had the slow, deliberate manner of a resigned bachelor. When Lyn arrived for dinner that evening, she immediately dismissed him as a possible suitor.

At one point, Morty watched Lyn as she adjusted the shoulder pads on her expensive silk blouse.

"They always put those things in the wrong places. They should just take them out," he suggested. Lyn couldn't help wondering what gave Morty—with his torn T-shirt and battered jacket—the idea that he could dispense fashion advice to anyone.

Despite their differences in style and temperament, Lyn and Morty had a pleasant evening, and Lyn thought that, in his own way, Morty was funny and charming enough—for someone. A couple of days later, Peggy called Lyn to see what she thought about Morty.

"Morty's all right," Lyn said, trying to be tactful. But she thought to herself: He's not what I'm looking for. He's short, he's nerdy, he's too much like Woody Allen. He doesn't have any of my must-have qualities.

"Don't you think he's funny?" Peggy cajoled her friend.

"I don't know."

"Come on, he's funny. Don't you think so?"

"I don't know, maybe."

The next day Peggy called Morty. She had a feeling about Lyn and Morty that she couldn't put her finger on.

"You've got to call Lyn," she told him. "She thinks you're really funny. She told me so, twice."

Morty was pleased and even a little surprised by the report, but he didn't rush to call Lyn, not wanting to appear over-anxious. Two weeks later, he finally phoned her office.

"This is Morty," he told Sal, Lyn's secretary.

"Just a minute please."

Sal came back on the line: "Were you involved in an accident?"

"No."

"Just a minute please."

A moment later she was back. "What is this regarding?"

"Tell her I'm the one she met," he said, his confidence waning, "at Peggy's house, at dinner."

But two weeks was a long time in Lyn's hectic world, and she had forgotten all about him. Still, she agreed to go out.

ALL LYN could remember about Morty was that he was short. The night he came to pick her up, Lyn was barefoot and in the middle of packing for her move into her new house. Boxes were strewn all over the apartment, and her cat was gliding through the maze.

Morty walked around her block four or five times until it was ten minutes past seven before he knocked on the door. Lyn answered on the second knock. Her cat slid out the door and crept between Morty's ankles.

"Hi," Morty said, awkwardly shuffling his feet.

His eyes, Lyn suddenly noticed, were an astonishing blue, Paul Newman blue.

"Your eyes," Lyn said, "they're so blue."

"Is that okay?" Morty asked.

But before she could respond, something bizarre happened: A flash of light protruded from his eyes and nearly knocked her down. Then, as she gathered her wits, a finger made of golden light appeared over Morty's head, pointing at him.

My God, she thought to herself, this is surreal. Lyn was not particularly religious, and she'd never had anything like this happen to her before, but the message was unmistakable: Someone or something was telling her that Morty was the guy for her. A voice in her head began to repeat, "This is the man you're going to marry."

Lyn was completely astonished and didn't know what to do. But as the voice and the vision persisted, she couldn't help arguing with it: No way, she thought, this can't be him. He's not tall, he doesn't play tennis. This can't be the guy.

The golden finger and the voice insisted that he was the guy.

In a daze, Lyn followed Morty to his dented Mazda as Morty opened the passenger door for her. Papers and empty coffee cups were strewn inside. Lyn removed a crumpled newspaper from the seat, her face screwed up in distaste, and ducked inside. As Morty got in, the golden finger still hovered above his head.

You've got to be kidding, she debated with the vision. This can't be the guy!

They went for dinner and then bowling, where Lyn, in a miniskirt, artfully bent low to toss the ball. They got along exceptionally well: Morty, an accountant, made her laugh all night long. The vision eventually subsided, but it lingered inside her. At one point in the evening, Morty gave Lyn a sweet kiss on the cheek, and she thought with automatic conviction, I'm going to marry this man. It did not seem a matter of choice: She knew—despite her lack of strong religious beliefs—that God had made it clear to her.

A few days later, they saw each other again, and Morty said, "I think we should take all our skeletons out of the closet."

"Fine," Lyn agreed. "You first."

They proceeded to tell each other their worst qualities. Oddly enough, Morty, who was wary of single women older than a certain age, saw himself as a good person who just fell through the cracks. Lyn, he felt, was another one.

Then he did something totally out of character: He took the bull by the horns.

"Well, we can do one of three things," Morty said. "We can carry our toothbrushes to each other's places. We can move in together. Or we can get married right away. I think we should get married."

Lyn was unfazed. "Fine. Let's get married," she said easily. She had thought of nothing else since their date. Morty impressed her by taking out a calendar; together they chose a date about two months away.

The next night Lyn met her family for dinner.

"I met the man I'm going to marry," Lyn said. She wasn't the least upset when her family responded as usual, "We're sick and tired of hearing about your men, Lyn. Just let us know when you're getting married."

Six days after their first date, Lyn and Morty were engaged; they married seven weeks later. A couple weeks after their first date, Lyn told Morty of her strange vision, but she has not had any similar visions since.

Today, Lyn has reduced her law practice and works side by side with Morty in a converted garage in the back of their home. They have two children—and an especially happy marriage.

Young Love

⌒

RICHARD WAS TEN years old the first time he laid eyes on Kathy. He had just finished playing a game of football, and he was watching the older team compete. Kathy, who was thirteen, was cheering for the opposition. She had stunning Mediterranean looks—an olive complexion and abundant dark hair. Her tan legs, extending from her white, pleated skirt, marched and kicked to a rap beat as she cheered her team to victory. Her dimples lit up her face whenever she laughed or smiled.

Richard, his eyes fixed on her, said to his teammates sitting next to him, "I'm going to marry her."

He sounded as serious as any ten-year-old can. His friends laughed: Kathy was beautiful—all the boys had crushes on her. What made Richard think he would ever have a chance with an older girl like her?

Richard's tightly knit Sicilian family lived in San Pedro, a vibrant harbor town in Southern California largely populated by descendants of Roman Catholic Italians and Yugoslavians. On Sundays, he went to church with his parents, his grandparents, and an aunt and uncle. Afterward, the family always shared a huge meal of homemade pasta and other Italian delicacies.

Richard might never have seen Kathy again—he was still in elementary school and she was three years older, in her last year in junior high. But a year after the football game, Kathy became best friends with his older sister, Desiree.

Kathy—who went to high school with Desiree—would come around Richard and Desiree's house almost every day. Whenever she was over, Richard tried to catch a glimpse of her irresistible smile. Soon, it was obvious that he had a crush on her, and she teased him mercilessly by pretending to flirt with him—treating him, not surprisingly, like her best friend's kid brother. When Desiree would mention a new girl Richard had met in school, Kathy would flash a dimple and say to him, "But I know you would rather be with me."

The teasing continued all through high school. "Who are those good-looking guys you're hanging out with?" she taunted him, referring to his friends in junior high. "Why don't you introduce me to the tall one with the blue eyes?" Richard felt his knees go weak. He thought to himself, What about me? I have blue eyes. But he tried never to let his true feelings show too much, even when Kathy's presence left him a little breathless.

For years he quietly endured her patronizing comments and brush-offs, serene in the knowledge that one day they would be together.

Eventually, Kathy went to college, and three years later Richard did the same. During this time, they saw each other only occasionally, usually on holidays when Kathy came over to visit Desiree. Once when Richard brought his college girlfriend home for Christmas, Kathy whispered to Desiree, "Doesn't she look just like me?"

Richard dated regularly in college, but he knew he would never marry any of those women. Without a plan or any reason to believe Kathy would ever return his affections, Richard nevertheless waited patiently for her.

Kathy was ambitious, smart, and restless—and she longed to see the world, to leave behind the longshoremen and the fishing docks and the insular community of San Pedro. She spent a semester at Harvard, graduated college, and interned in Washington, D.C., at the U.S. Department of Education. After that, she decided to earn a teaching credential at a university near San Pedro, but she planned eventually to settle somewhere else, New York or Boston perhaps. East Coast cities were exciting and culturally stimulating, and she was determined not to marry anyone from her hometown.

Now in her mid-twenties, Kathy dated with more caution than she had as an undergraduate. She was tired of waiting for men who said, "I'll call you," and never called, and one relationship she had with a man in Boston ended particularly badly when she discovered he hadn't been faithful.

After she earned her teaching credential, Kathy took a substitute teaching job in a nearby school. On her first day, the principal of San Pedro Elementary School called the principal at the school where Kathy was substituting. He mentioned that they had an immediate opening for a teacher and inquired whether anyone there might be suitable.

"I have a substitute here today who appears very competent," his colleague said, and he mentioned Kathy. Because securing a teaching position in the highly regarded San Pedro school district was considered a coup, Kathy agreed to an interview and put aside her plans to see the world: She got the job and started teaching in San Pedro the very next Monday. She taught for one year, and then for another year after that. She was the maid of honor at Desiree's wedding, and she was the first friend Desiree told when she found out she was pregnant.

Meanwhile, Richard graduated from the University of Arizona and returned to San Pedro, settling into his boyhood room in his parents' home. He got a job working for a real estate developer. Richard was content to return to San Pedro to be close to his family and lifelong friends, and, when the time came, to start his own branch of the clan.

Desiree now lived in San Diego, and after her son was born, she would come home to visit for a few days at a time. It gave Richard a chance to see Kathy, who came over to visit Desiree and the baby whenever they were in town. Kathy laughed good-naturedly when she saw Richard playing with his nephew, cuddling him, giving him his bottle, and mimicking his baby faces. She thought to herself, I have never seen a man so gentle with a baby.

"You're all grown up now, Richard," she said, her smile sincere. The next few times they saw each other, Richard noticed that her teasing flirtations had mellowed and become ever-so-slightly more serious.

In fact, when Richard showed up at his nephew's baptism with his girlfriend of six months, Kathy was surprised. During the ceremony, Kathy kept glancing over at him huddled next to his girlfriend, and she felt, for the first time, something close to jealously. At the party after the ceremony, Kathy took Richard aside. "Why did you bring her here?" she asked.

"She's my girlfriend," he replied evenly.

Inside, he was ecstatic that Kathy had noticed. Richard was now twenty-five, and he was content to build his career; he wasn't yet ready for marriage. But Kathy's gripe about his girlfriend was the opening he had waited for since he was ten years old.

As people toasted the new baby, and the family and guests feasted, Richard devised his first mischievous plot to spend some time alone with Kathy: He decided to get his girlfriend drunk. For the next couple of hours, he refilled her glass with beer, champagne, and then vodka, which she drank happily, caught up in the celebration. Finally, she said to Richard, "I feel like I'm going to pass out."

"I'll take you home," he said. After he drove her home and put her to bed, Richard charged back to the party to find Kathy.

Two weeks later, Richard invited Kathy to drive with him to San Diego to visit Desiree. In the car, she suddenly realized that after knowing each other for fifteen years, this was the first time they had ever been alone together. Kathy wasn't sure how to feel: Richard had always been like a younger brother to her—but now he was also handsome, attentive, and endearing.

Later that day, as they gave way to their romantic feelings, they kissed for the first time. With a nervous laugh, Kathy said, "I feel like I'm kissing my kid brother. Don't you feel kind of strange?"

Richard looked at her incredulously. The thought never crossed his mind. "This just feels right," he said.

After that, they began dating officially, and they were engaged a year and a half later. After Kathy had accepted his proposal, Richard told her he knew he was going to marry her when he was ten years old, the first time he saw her, and had even said so then.

"But all the boys liked me then," Kathy said.

"But I knew, I always knew I was going to marry you."

In 1996, they married in Richard's family's church in San Pedro, where they still live. Today, Kathy is still teaching at San Pedro Elementary School, and Richard works as a mortgage broker.

I Can See Forever

~

*I*T WAS A Thursday afternoon and Tiffany was on her way
to the mall to buy a birthday present for her brother. Traffic was
fairly light on Madison Avenue, one of suburban Sacramento's
major thoroughfares. Tiffany switched the radio station, humming along to a pop tune. She slowed to a stop as the light
turned red.

Just then a shiny BMW came to an abrupt halt beside her.
Tiffany turned to look and stopped humming. All in an instant,
her eyes locked with the handsome, young driver's, and something inexplicable happened. Tiffany felt she was not merely
meeting the other man's eyes, but, in fact, was seeing *through*
them—that she was somehow, for a moment, part of him.
Usually outgoing and outspoken, Tiffany's normal reaction
when she saw a boy looking at her might have been to wave or
call out, but she could only look away demurely, awed by the
strange, powerful experience.

The light turned green and Tiffany, slightly trembling,
changed her course. She veered to the right and headed to her
parents' house just up ahead. Meanwhile, the driver of the

BMW attempted to follow her, making an illegal U-turn in the process, but he lost sight of her when she pulled her car into her parents' driveway, disappearing from the road

Tiffany jumped out of the car, slammed the door, and ran into the house. "Mom!" she shouted. "Mom!"

Tiffany was seventeen and about to start classes at the local junior college on Monday. She was naturally cheerful and gregarious, slim and pretty with dark blond hair, shining brown eyes, and refined features.

"Mom, I just saw the cutest guy I've ever seen in my whole life!"

"Really? Where?"

"At a stoplight."

"A stoplight? Did you exchange numbers?"

"No, but it was the most amazing thing!"

"Tiffany," her mom said, "why are you so worked up over this? You're probably never going to see him again."

"I don't know. I just can't explain it."

Later, Tiffany recounted the story to her best friend. "It was the most incredible moment."

"This is dumb," her friend said. "You'll never see him again. Forget about it."

RON, THE driver of the BMW, had had a similar powerful experience at the stoplight, and he felt an incalculable loss when Tiffany's car disappeared around the corner. Born in the Philippines, Ron was also seventeen, and he had moved with his family as a young child first to Chicago and then to Sacramento. Later that same evening he told his brother, "I saw the cutest girl I've ever seen."

"Where?"

"At a stoplight."

"Did you get her number?"

"No. But I'm going to drive down Madison Avenue every day at the same time until I find her."

His brother smirked, "Good luck!"

"I've got to find her," Ron replied, determined.

The following Monday, Tiffany had her first day at junior college. As she was pulling out of her parking space after classes, she saw Ron's BMW, moving slowly at first, then suddenly making an illegal left turn toward her car. Ron inched past her, and they glanced quickly at one another and kept going, too afraid to stop and talk. Tiffany gasped, That's him! He goes to school here!

Ron was enrolled at the same school, but for the first couple of days he did not go to any of his classes. Instead, he stood in the halls or outside buildings, waiting for Tiffany to exit a classroom until he had memorized her schedule. Ron would watch her—surrounded by her friends, slim and graceful, her hair glistening in the sun and bouncing as she walked—but every time, he lost his nerve and never approached her. Her friends saw him lurking in the halls and told her, "He was here again today." Tiffany wondered how long this would go on.

For two weeks, Ron continued approaching and retreating, until one afternoon they ran into each other in the school parking lot. Tiffany couldn't stand the suspense any longer, and she was just about to shout out when Ron approached her car.

"I just want to know your name," he said.

"It's Tiffany." She giggled with relief. She was glad to have finally met him.

The next day they had coffee together. They were both teenagers with little dating experience, but after that first cup of coffee, they dated exclusively. They both knew that they would get married—when the time was right. While their friends traveled in and out of relationships, Ron and Tiffany were always together.

In 1994, six years after they met at the stoplight, they married in a historic Sacramento church. They still live in Sacramento, where they are raising their daughter.

Before they were married, Tiffany's friends would sometimes ask, "How can you be so sure that Ron is right for you?"

She would always reply, "When I look in his eyes, I can see forever."

Resolution

~

$\mathcal{D}$O NOT INTRODUCE to me to any more men," Debra told her girlfriends one day. "And I don't mean to be rude, but I don't want to hear about your dates either."

After years of marathon dating—sometimes three or four dates in a single day—Debra swore off men one Friday in February 1996. At thirty-one, she was beginning to wonder whether she was meant to be married. A teacher with genuine warmth, New York spunk, and a slight Long Island accent, Debra privately believed that in matters of the heart a person just knew when he or she had met the right one. And as yet, she hadn't.

The next day, Debra visited her parents on Long Island. On Saturday night, she went dancing with a girlfriend at a nearby club. When two men approached, she shooed them away, pulled her girlfriend to the dance floor, and danced with abandon, enjoying the freedom of her recent emancipation from dating.

Sunday, she suffered a fierce allergic reaction to her parents' new cat. Her eyes watered and swelled up, her nose turned bright red, and her pearly skin broke out in blotches. As the day wore on, she could barely breathe. Her friend Linda, who was visiting, urged her to take the train back with her to Manhattan that night.

"You know I never go home on Sunday nights," Debra declared, sniffling as she removed her clothes from the dryer.

"Come on, just this once."

"No. I never go Sunday, and I hate taking the night train. I always take an early train on Monday." She placed a neatly folded towel on the pile.

"I don't want to go alone," Linda said. "Please."

Debra sneezed and rubbed her eyes. "This cat is driving me crazy!" After a minute she looked at Linda. "Oh, all right, I'll go back with you tonight, but only because I can't stand these allergies. I don't think they've ever been this bad."

"Great!" Linda skipped out of the room. "I'll pick you up at eight."

"Yeah, yeah," Debra muttered, continuing to fold and stack her laundry.

IN A local diner elsewhere on Long Island, a man named Jack was also thinking about getting back to Manhattan as he finished dinner with his parents.

The waitress came over, her pad resting in her palm. "You folks want some carrot cake or apple pie?"

"No, thank you," Jack said. "I've got a 7:30 train to catch."

"Yeah, but dessert comes with your specials. Coffee or tea, too."

"That's okay. No thanks."

"You don't want your dessert?" the waitress said incredulously.

Jack's mother said to him, "Come on, let's have some dessert. You'll catch the 8:30." Then, before her son could respond, she added, "We get to spend another hour with you."

"All right," Jack said, giving in.

A few minutes before 8:30, Jack and his parents arrived at the train station. From the back seat of his parents' car, Jack caught sight of Debra—tall, slender, good-looking—talking with Linda and dabbing her nose with a tissue. In addition to her overnight bag and purse, Debra carried a large sack bulging with a week's worth of laundry.

Jack suddenly thought to himself, "I want to get to know her." He grabbed his bag, said good-bye to his parents, and followed Debra onto the train, taking a seat across from her.

Debra, still coughing and sneezing, asked a man sitting nearby if she could borrow his paper. As Debra began flipping through the various sections, Linda elbowed her.

"Look up," she whispered. "There's this incredibly good-looking guy looking over at you."

"Please. I'm not in the mood," Debra said, closing her watery eyes for a minute. "Remember, no men, so leave me alone."

Debra went back to the paper. But several minutes later, she couldn't help stealing a glance at Jack. She returned to her paper, silently indicating that she agreed with Linda's assessment, but Debra resolved to take no further notice. After all, she had made a pact with herself.

For the next forty-five minutes, Jack kept glancing at Debra and trying to think of a natural way to start a conversation. As the moments ticked by and nothing came to him, he became increasingly distraught.

Five minutes before they rolled into Penn Station, Jack leaned forward awkwardly and asked, "What are you looking for in the paper?"

"I don't know," she answered, looking at him over the top of a page. Then she added, "I won't know until I find it." The words had spilled forth as if they had a life of their own, taking Debra by surprise; *she* didn't even really know what she'd meant by them.

As they disembarked at Penn Station, Debra chatted with Linda amid the tumult of people arriving and departing. Jack caught up with her and asked, "Would you like to go out for dinner or a drink—"

"Oh, sure," Debra answered immediately, struggling with her sack of laundry and turning back to Linda to say good-bye.

"—sometime?" Jack finished saying. But Debra hadn't heard him.

Debra turned back to Jack and handed him her bulky laundry bag. "Let's drop this at my apartment first."

Jack's face screwed up in a confused expression. Noticing his bewilderment, Debra turned around and mouthed to Linda, "He's weird." Then she nodded her head to confirm that this was the reason she made her no-dating resolution, just two days earlier.

Jack, carrying the cumbersome bag, followed Debra to her apartment. As Debra went to freshen up in the bathroom, she suddenly realized to her horror that she had let an absolute stranger into her apartment. She quickly combed her hair, came out of the bathroom, and grabbed her purse. "Let's go," she said abruptly. Jack couldn't figure out what was going on.

But at the café, they both relaxed and their conversation flowed pleasantly. They had a real and immediate rapport. After a while, Jack admitted: "I think you're so adorable," he said. "But I didn't ask you out tonight."

Debra's eyes widened in surprise. "You didn't?"

"No. I didn't. I asked if you wanted to go out *sometime*."

"Oops." Debra turned red with embarrassment.

Jack smiled, saying earnestly, "But I'm glad we're here."

Debra was, too, and they continued talking that night until 3:30 A.M. When they finally parted, Jack said with a conviction that would have seemed unbelievable to him six hours before, "This is very serious. We're going to get married."

Debra was charmed and a little swept away, but she reminded herself that this was New York, and guys often said things they didn't mean.

"I'll call you for lunch tomorrow," he promised.

And he did, despite his tendency to hang back and just let things happen. Rather than pursue things, he usually let things pursue him. Jack was a Wall Street stockbroker, but he disliked trading—it was a stressful job that at times felt vaguely inhuman—and he'd found that it was at odds with his naturally mild temperament. But from the moment he saw Debra, he felt mysteriously propelled toward her, and he pursued her with unusual dedication.

They had lunch and dinner every day after their first date. Two weeks later, when Debra introduced Jack to her parents, he told them he planned to marry her. To her surprise, Debra realized that the way she felt about Jack was the way she had

always dreamed of feeling about a man—and so much for res-
olutions. Two weeks after Jack's declaration to her parents,
they became engaged. They married in October 1996—just
eight months after Debra had sworn off men—and they still
live in New York City. Debra is now writing scripts, and Jack
no longer works on Wall Street.

A Stranger on the Bus

$\sim$

BEFORE DINNER ONE Friday, Tina was in her room, putting her clothes away and organizing her books and papers. She was eighteen, a senior in high school, and she would start college in the fall. Every so often, she paused and stared blankly at the walls, feeling restless.

Tina appeared suddenly in the kitchen, where her mother was preparing dinner. "Mom, I want to go visit Aunt Florence and Uncle Michael."

"Well, we'll see about planning a trip there in a month."

"No, Mom," Tina insisted. "I want to go this weekend."

"This weekend?" her mother said, laughing. "I can't possibly get organized—"

"I want to go alone."

Her mother looked up from her chopping. Tina was serious about her strange request.

"But we always go as a family to see them. You know, make it like a vacation. You've never gone alone before."

"I know. But I just feel like going. I'm perfectly able to go alone. I'm going to college soon—I'll have to do things on my own."

Her mother shook her head. "I don't know. This seems so out of the ordinary."

Tina pressed some more, and her mother, seeing no good reason to refuse, gave her consent. Tina gave her a quick kiss on the cheek.

"Thank you." She turned to go. "I'll go pack."

The next day, Tina was on the bus headed to her relatives' house. Within half an hour, the drab city landscape had given way to gently sloping mountains and trees green in the full bloom of summer. Tina took out a book to read but had difficulty concentrating, going over the same paragraph three times without comprehending it. The bus was practically empty, and she watched distractedly at each stop as people got on and off. Then a young man in his late twenties boarded and took a seat behind the driver.

Tina put her book aside. It was no use. She watched the young man, who looked foreign. He seemed to be of average appearance, with dark hair and eyes, and from time to time, he would ask the bus driver questions.

As she watched him, the strangest feeling came over her. She felt herself being pulled toward him. Out of the blue, she thought, I'm going to marry this man. A more rational voice interjected: But I don't know him. I've never said a word to him. Nonetheless, the magnetic force remained. Where is he from? she wondered. What is he talking to the bus driver about? Wrapped up in her thoughts, she was startled when she noticed he was getting off the bus.

"Oh!" she gasped out loud. She looked out the window, craning to see as he walked away. She felt extremely disappointed. What a pity, she thought.

Tina got off the bus one stop later and headed toward her uncle's house. Her heart beat rapidly. She could not shake the odd feeling. She kissed her aunt and uncle hello, gave them the update on everyone in her family, and then they all settled into the living room.

Tina could not contain her thoughts any longer.

"The strangest thing happened on the bus over here!" Tina exclaimed, and she began to tell them what had happened. As she was speaking, there was a knock on the door. Uncle Michael excused himself while Tina and her aunt continued to talk. Male voices echoed in the foyer, growing louder and more distinct as the two men entered the living room. Tina turned to see who it was. My God! she thought, her eyes opening wide.

To her aunt, she leaned over and whispered, "That's him! The man I have been telling you about on the bus!" Tina couldn't believe he was standing there in front of her, and she beamed with happiness. He must have gotten off one stop too soon, she thought.

"Tina," Uncle Michael said, "this is my second cousin James. He's visiting us from Iran for a week."

Like Uncle Michael, James was a dentist, and he worked for the Iranian army, which had given him a couple months' leave. After his stay in America, he was headed for a three-week vacation in Europe.

Tina and James spent the evening talking, and Tina again felt the same magnetic pull between them. Until that day, she had not thought of marriage—she was only just off to college—but she felt certain that one day she would marry this man.

James was also drawn to Tina. In the week he stayed with Uncle Michael, he and Tina saw each other as much as they could. During his trip to Europe, James sent Tina presents from every city he visited. Later, James's best friend—who was also his European traveling companion—told Tina, "James was so excited about meeting you that he couldn't sleep."

That fall, Tina started college and James eventually returned to Iran. They corresponded for ten months, until he finished his stint in the Iranian army and moved to the United States permanently. Tina and James were engaged shortly after he returned; they married a year after that, in 1976. Today, they live in California and have three children.

PART SEVEN

Matchmaker, Matchmaker

MATCHMAKING *is still one of the most common ways for people to meet. In some cultures, families still use professional matchmakers to find suitable spouses for their children. But a matchmaker can be anyone who has a hand in bringing two people together. In these stories, the matchmakers are friends, family members, and even coworkers. Sometimes they, too, act based on intuition or a sign, prompting them to introduce two people who never would have met without their intervention.*

Pleasure Reading

⌒

$\mathcal{A}$s GERALD WAITED for Andrew to finish getting ready to go out, he looked around his friend's living room. He examined the books neatly lined up on the shelf, scanning the titles: medical books, a few best-sellers, and some worn books with "Used" stickers still attached, probably required reading for his undergraduate medical school courses. An unusual title caught his attention. He pulled the book from the shelf: *The Man Who Mistook His Wife for a Hat,* by Oliver Sacks. How peculiar, Gerald thought.

He leafed through the pages, skimming the text and stopping here and there to read a paragraph or two. The book contained short stories of neurological case histories that emphasized the human side of medical professionals and their extraordinary patients. It was just like Andrew to have a book like this, Gerald thought. Andrew was in his last year of medical school, and he already displayed the compassionate understanding of an excellent doctor, one who would later be known for his exceptional bedside manner.

Andrew came into the room, his hair still wet. "Okay, let's go."

As Gerald shelved the volume, Andrew commented, "That's a great book. I read it twice. You can borrow it if you want."

"That's okay," said Gerald. "I already looked through it."

Several weeks later, Gerald was visiting his friend Julie at her apartment. He noticed a familiar book on her coffee table—the same book he had thumbed through at Andrew's: *The Man Who Mistook His Wife for a Hat*. That's strange, he thought. I've never even heard of the book, and now I've seen it twice in just a few weeks.

Julie was a physiotherapist who used biofeedback methods to rehabilitate her patients, and Gerald thought that maybe the book had something to do with her work. But the coincidence stirred something in him. The next day he called Andrew.

"There's a girl I think you should meet." He related the coincidence.

"Just because we have the same book?" Andrew asked.

"It's not your typical book. Anyway, she's cute." Gerald persisted, unable to adequately explain why he thought they should meet or why owning the same book was significant. It just felt that way.

"Gerald, I'm still seeing Lisa," Andrew said. "But thanks for thinking of me."

However, as Gerald knew, things with Lisa and Andrew were not working out. And in fact, six months later, they broke up.

Gerald could not get the match out of his head. One evening not long after the breakup, Gerald pursued his suggestion with Andrew again. "I think you should go out with Julie," he said on the phone.

"Who?" Andrew said.

"You know, the girl with the book."

"What book?" Andrew asked, a bit impatient.

"The Man Who Mistook His Wife for a Hat," Gerald said, grinning to himself.

"All right, all right, enough with the book. I'll meet her."

When Gerald finally introduced Andrew and Julie in February 1994, the pair connected immediately: There was an instant attraction. They dated for a few months, were engaged that August, and married in October that same year. Today, they have two children, and they remain dedicated to each other and their respective professions. One day Andrew and Julie hope to open a health clinic together.

Mr. Tan Makes a Match

⌒

IN THE 1940S, Jennifer and John's grandparents, fleeing the political intolerance of China, all escaped to Taiwan in the wake of the Chinese Revolution. As a result, Jennifer and John's parents grew up in Taiwan, but they didn't meet each other until all four became college students at the University of Oregon at Eugene. Returning to Taiwan, both couples married, and then they both moved to the United States permanently in the 1960s. Eventually, both couples moved to California, where they settled and started their families.

Their children often played together. John's father would pinch Jennifer's cheek and say, "You two should get married one day." As a child, she hated the sting his pinch left on her face and found the idea of marriage repugnant. Jennifer was the only girl among the group of several boys, of whom John was the oldest. After a few years, John's family moved to the far side of the city and the two families lost touch.

Two decades passed. Jennifer's family were devout Christians, her mother an ordained minister. The family attended church every Sunday, and they were active in their community. They wore their faith naturally, and they turned to God often—for help, for advice, for a sign. One Sunday, just as Jennifer and her family were about to leave for church, the phone rang. Jennifer's dad answered it.

"Hello, this is Ron Tan," the man on the line said. The voice was familiar, but Jennifer's father couldn't place it.

"This is John and Ken's father," the voice said.

"Ron!" Jennifer's father exclaimed, suddenly recognizing his old friend. "What a surprise! It's been such a long time."

"Twenty years," Mr. Tan replied.

"Twenty years," Jennifer's father repeated softly, trying to comprehend how so many years could pass so quickly. "Good to hear from you," he said graciously. "How's everyone?" He wondered what had prompted Ron to call now, out of the blue.

"Just fine," Mr. Tan said. "Listen, can we come to your church today?"

It seemed an odd request, since the Tans lived quite a distance away, but Jennifer's father simply responded, "Of course. It'll be good to see you." He hung up the phone and turned to his wife. "You won't believe who that was."

Before the church service, Jennifer saw her mom standing outside.

"What are you doing out here, Mom?"

"I'm waiting for the Tans to arrive."

Of course, Jennifer thought; she had forgotten they were coming. An image of Mr. Tan teasing her about marrying John suddenly popped into her head.

At lunch after the services, Jennifer was reintroduced to the

Tans, who had come without their children. As she turned to leave, Mr. Tan said, "Why don't you get together with John sometime?"

Jennifer turned red. Here he was, in front of everyone, treating her like she was six years old again and still trying to get them together. She remained polite, but inside she seethed. She wasn't interested in Mr. Tan's matchmaking. She was twenty-seven, smart, self-reliant, with a graduate degree in sociology and a job at a cutting-edge marketing firm. She had no trouble meeting men, and in fact, she had an extreme aversion to being set up—even by friends and others she trusted. Blind dates always felt unnatural and awkward.

She recalled a time when her grandmother had said, "Your uncle who works at Boeing knows many nice Chinese boys. They are engineers. He can introduce you."

"If you want to do something for me Grandma, then pray for me," Jennifer retorted. She had dated all sorts of men with a variety of ethnic backgrounds. Her only requirement was that the men she dated must hold God central in their lives, the way she did.

The year before, Jennifer had experienced a terrible breakup with a long-term boyfriend. She was tired of dating the wrong men and had resigned the matter to God. She had not dated for more than a year, believing that the right one would come along if God had planned it for her.

As Jennifer stood there blushing red and holding her tongue, her mother gently suggested that she go along with it. The Tans had just been speaking very highly of their son John to them in the church. Then, completely out of character, Jennifer yielded. She ran to her car in the rain to find a business card to give to Mr. Tan as her brothers watched in amazement.

Later, Jennifer prayed for clarity on the matter—her behavior had so confused her. "God," she asked, "if John is the one for me, let him call in the next few days."

LITTLE DID Jennifer know, John resented his father's efforts as much as she did. John was completing an internship in oncology. He worked 120-hour weeks and didn't want to waste his precious spare time. John had always found women to date without anyone's help; he had never had his dad make an introduction before. I'm not going to call, John thought.

Seeing his son's reluctance, John's father kept bugging him.

"Fine, I'll call, when I have time," he said to please his father, thinking to himself, Not for a few weeks, I'm just too busy. But after a day or so, a strange urge prompted John to call. He dialed Jennifer's number, and she answered on the second ring.

He said, "Hi, is this Jennifer?"

"Yes. It's me." Jennifer was surprised at how relieved she felt.

"This is John Tan. My dad gave me your number."

They talked for a while and discovered they had attended the same university at the same time. They knew so many of the same people it was unusual that they had not met before— that is, since they were little children. Despite their many connections, foremost in Jennifer's mind was whether John was religious. She didn't want a Christian in name or by birth only; she wanted someone who lived and practiced Christian teaching.

They began talking about John's work at the hospital. He

told her he had just finished treating a terminal cancer patient.

"We did all we could for her," he told Jennifer. "There was nothing more I could do, medically. So I turned her over to God and prayed."

Jennifer's heart skipped a beat. She could not have written a more perfect script. Her mind became free of doubts, and she later realized it was at that moment she decided she had found the right man. They spoke for two and half hours and made tentative plans to go out Saturday night.

Jennifer could not help reflecting on the long path taken by their grandparents, who had fled Communist China to preserve their beliefs, which had led to this. Perhaps Mr. Tan had allowed himself some harmless meddling because he sensed that their union was the last leg of their families' common destiny.

Jennifer prepared for their date on Saturday night convinced that John would be her husband, and the final turn of events confirmed her belief.

John had warned Jennifer that he was on call at the hospital all day on Saturday, and that if he was called in—which was highly likely—he'd have to cancel their plans at the last minute. But all afternoon John didn't hear a peep from the hospital, and at one point he even checked his pager to make sure it was working. That had never happened before. Then, sure enough, an hour before he was to go out, the pager went off.

John called the hospital, certain that he would have to cancel his date. A child needed radiation treatment, and he spoke to the physician who was the child's internist.

"Do you have plans tonight?" the doctor asked John.

"Yes, but—" John was not one to shirk responsibility.

"You go ahead with whatever you have planned," the internist said. "I've got a lot of work to do here anyway. I'll administer the treatment."

John was astonished. In all his years of residency, he had never received such an offer.

John and Jennifer went on their date, undisturbed the whole evening. Jennifer thought John looked exactly as he did when they had played as children. There was not a moment of awkwardness between them. In 1998, a year later, they became engaged.

An Accidental Meeting

~

$\mathcal{D}$EBBIE STOOD NEAR the hors d'oeuvres and scanned the room for eligible bachelors. She was attending the company Christmas party of her friend Karen, and they had made their way over to the extravagant food display. Debbie helped herself to the salmon mousse.

"Try the stuffed mushrooms," Karen said, a mushroom in her hand. "They're incredible. I've got to learn how they make these. My husband loves mushrooms."

"Yeah, well, you've got someone to cook for," Debbie said. "It's no fun cooking for one."

Debbie was thirty-two, a successful radio producer. She had moved from New York to the West Coast for work, but at heart she remained a spunky, assertive New Yorker. For some time she had wanted to marry someone and settle down, and the feeling was always strongest around the holidays.

"Let's get a drink," Debbie suggested. On their way to the bar, Debbie spotted a handsome man with curly, dark hair and a short beard. Something about how he wore his well-cut suit made her romanticize that, despite his formal appearance, he probably liked hiking and picnics at the beach.

"Do you know him?" Debbie asked, pointing him out to Karen.

"No, never seen him."

"He's *very* cute."

Just then, Jeff, a mutual friend, walked over to join them.

"Hi, ladies," Jeff said. "Enjoying yourselves? I could use one of those." He eyed Karen's drink.

"I wonder if he's single," Debbie said, still watching the attractive stranger.

"Who?" Jeff asked.

"That one over there," Karen said, motioning with her head. "Jeff, why don't you go introduce yourself. See if he wants to meet Debbie."

"No!" Debbie shrieked. "You can't do that!"

"But you want to meet him. Jeff would be perfect—"

"What if he's married?" Debbie cut her off.

"He's not acting married," Karen observed. "Come on, Jeff."

Jeff prepared to go on Debbie's signal. "No, wait. Oh, I don't know," she said.

As Debbie wrestled with her indecision, the attractive stranger walked away, disappearing into the party. Debbie looked so disappointed that Jeff promised if he ever saw him again, that he would make an attempt to introduce himself.

Debbie went home that night still feeling disappointed. She brushed her teeth, washed off her makeup, and looked wistfully into the mirror. "You blew it," she said out loud. In her bedroom, she pulled back the covers and slid into bed. She comforted herself with the thought that he'd left before she'd had a chance to meet him, but the missed opportunity haunted her for days.

Two months later, Jeff and Karen attended a sales and marketing seminar with a large contingent of associates from their company. They were standing near the snack table during a break when Karen tugged at Jeff's shirt. "That's him! That's him!" she whispered.

"That's who?" Jeff asked.

"The guy Debbie wanted to meet at the Christmas party." He had the same type of brown, curly hair, the same short beard, and was well-dressed.

"You've got to go over and talk to him. Debbie never forgave herself for not letting you introduce her the first time."

"What if he's not available?"

"Go talk to him," she said, pushing him gently. "You'll soon find out."

Jeff walked over to the stranger.

"Hi, my name is Jeff," he said. They shook hands.

"Tom."

Jeff talked to him for a few minutes about the seminar, about their work, getting a feel for his personality. When Tom turned out to be polite, articulate, and interesting, he decided to reveal his true purpose.

"This may sound a little strange," Jeff began, "but a friend of mine wanted to meet you at the Christmas party. She saw you from across the room. She's a good friend of mine—she's a wonderful woman." Jeff paused a minute to gauge Tom's interest. He did not interrupt, so Jeff continued. "She's a successful radio producer from New York. You know, a lot of energy. She's great."

"Then why don't you go out with her?" Tom asked.

Oh, he's single all right, Jeff thought. Then he said, "I met her years ago when I was dating someone else pretty seriously, and I've always known her as a friend. We're really like brother and sister. Anyway, she saw you at the Christmas party and found you attractive."

"What Christmas party?" he asked.

"The one the firm threw this past Christmas."

"I didn't go to any company Christmas party."

"Oh," Jeff said, surprised. "Excuse me, I thought you had." He turned around, looking for Karen. "I was sure you were the guy she saw at the party. I'm really sorry." Jeff shrugged, not sure what to do. He had enjoyed talking to Tom, who seemed interested in hearing about Debbie.

"Well, maybe you would like to meet her anyway?" Jeff asked.

"Sure. But she wanted to go out with the other guy. She may not be interested."

"Don't worry about that. You seem like her type."

"Great. I'm from New York myself," Tom said. They talked for another fifteen minutes, until it was time for the seminar to resume, and Jeff told him all about Debbie. Before they went to take their seats, Jeff handed Tom her telephone number.

Jeff got home late that night, but he called Debbie anyway.

"Everything okay?" she asked, her voice sleepy.

"Yes, fine. You're not going to believe this. Remember the guy from the Christmas party you wanted to meet?"

"Yeah . . ."

"Well, at the seminar tonight, Karen and I ran into a guy—"

"You ran into the guy from the Christmas party? That's amazing," Debbie said excitedly, perking up immediately. "Did you mention me?"

"Well, yeah—listen—this one is from New York."

"New York!" Debbie squealed. "I can't believe it. He's from New York! You know I love guys from New York!"

"Debbie, wait—"

"Did you give him my number?"

"I did. But I've been trying to tell you, he wasn't the one from the party."

"What?" Her voice dropped.

"Karen thought it was the guy from the party—so I went over and talked to him. He did look a lot like the other guy. But it turns out he never went to the party. We got the wrong guy."

"You're kidding."

"No, I'm not. We talked for a while. He seems like a great guy—definitely your type. I think you should meet him."

"He wants to meet me?"

"Yeah. I told him all about you. I gave him your number."

"You gave him my number? Are you sure you checked him out?" Debbie said, whose hopes were rising again.

"I had a good feeling about him," Jeff assured her.

A couple of days later, Tom called. They had a very pleasant talk and arranged to meet—and Debbie found herself looking forward to it a great deal more than she had expected.

When Tom picked up Debbie at her apartment, they exchanged genuine smiles.

"You do sort of look like the other guy," Debbie observed.

"You're the third person who's said that," Tom said, smiling.

Tom was thirty-seven. They were both smart professionals, and long past the age of fleeting infatuations, yet they both sensed an immediate attraction. After three minutes, Tom said later, he knew that he would marry her. Debbie felt so comfortable with him she swore it seemed as if she had known Tom her whole life.

They became engaged after only two weeks. They married in 1990 and now have two children.

SOMETIME AFTER Debbie and Tom married, Karen pulled Jeff aside. "You know," she said, "I knew Tom wasn't the same guy from the Christmas party."

"What?!" Jeff howled.

"But I could tell he was Debbie's type. And if I told you it was the guy from the Christmas party, I knew you'd go over to him, because you promised Debbie you would."

Jeff gave her a stern look, not appreciating her ruse.

"Well, it was worth it, wasn't it?" she asked.

Suddenly, Jeff smiled. "Looks that way," he said, shaking his head over the unusual and unlikely chain of events.

PART EIGHT

The Power of Suggestion

THE *act of expressing ourselves is incredibly powerful. Giving voice to our desires—shaping through words and art the abstract and seemingly insubstantial complexity of our emotional and spiritual lives—makes them real. By doing so we create our reality and give it meaning.*

When we speak from our hearts to unburden, console, or persuade, we can't help but be changed by the experience. Our lives become richer as our inner essence is revealed. In these stories, each partner's creative expression of his or her thoughts and feelings is the key to bringing the other partner closer.

Letters

⌒

IN 1983, DONNA was home on Christmas break in Hartford, Ohio, a rural country laid with fertile fields and dotted by large, old farmhouses topped with shingle roofs. Reading the local paper one morning, Donna came across a very moving letter from a teacher, who wrote about his brother, a military chaplain currently stationed in Beirut. Two months earlier, two hundred U.S. Marines had been killed when a militant Lebanese suicide bomber drove a truck full of explosives into their compound. The tragedy had been all over the news at the time, and the letter was meant as a brief reminder of the service personnel overseas, who were still struggling with the tragedy. The chaplain's address was provided.

Later, Donna got out one of her Christmas cards. Addressing the letter to no one in particular, she wrote:

Dear Marine,
    Merry Christmas and Happy New Year. I want to let you know that you are in our thoughts and prayers back home.

In February, unexpectedly, Donna received an answer. The letter was handwritten on military stationery. The letter writer's script was neat and small:

> Dear Donna,
>
> Thank you for your Christmas greeting. It brings us much comfort to know that people back home are thinking about us. My platoon was recently in Grenada during the United States' invasion. We were able to secure the small island, and afterward we were sent to Beirut as part of a peacekeeping mission. But our presence here is far from safe.

He told her that they lived in bunkers dug deep in the ground and were in constant danger of sniper and rocket fire. *Please write back,* the marine wrote at the end of the letter and signed it: *Corporal George McLean.*

Donna wrote back:

> Dear Corporal McLean,
>
> Your response to my letter came as an unexpected surprise. I learned about the bombing when I was in school at the University of Akron. It was a shock to everyone. I'm in my junior year and am majoring in business and computer science. I was home in Hartford with my family during Christmas when I mailed the card.

She wrote some more about her family. How did you get my letter? she asked before signing off.

George wrote back again. Using short, direct sentences, he

told her about his life as a marine. He wrote of everyday things, like where they slept and the relentless desert heat:

They fly us out by helicopter once every two weeks to naval aircraft to shower, since rocket fire destroyed our shower near the bunker. The bunkers are dirty; rats run through them all the time. We even named one little guy who likes to hang around a lot.

Donna wrote back again. They became pen pals.

George and Donna wrote dutifully to each other; their letters maintained a tone of respectful friendship. For George, Donna's letters brought him the sweet feel of home amid the dirt, heat, and boredom of the desert. But even more, he confided in Donna in a way that he could not confide in his fellow marines. Looking for the Ohio postmark, he would carefully separate her letters from his other mail; he didn't read them until he could be alone. Her correspondence was usually sunny: chatty tidbits about her day, her studies, and sorority events—although she tried to downplay it, her carefree, comfortable life came through. Before signing her name she always wrote: *I hope you are taking care of yourself and are keeping safe.*

Donna would also send George an occasional humor card, and when she went home for school breaks, she sent him cookies she had baked herself. For Easter she mailed some chocolate bunnies, causing a minor fracas among George's fellow marines. Donna occasionally wrote on stationery adorned with rose petals or maple leaves. The paper seemed to him especially delicate and fragile. George always thanked Donna for her packages and cards, but she never knew the extent to which her small acts of kindness were seeing him through his tour of duty.

Donna was a smart, young woman; she studied hard and dated often. Her outgoing, optimistic temperament came, in part, from a loving, supportive family who genuinely enjoyed spending time together. After a while, George's letters—his firsthand accounts of a soldier's life in active duty—became an important part of her life. They sometimes arrived two at a time, and she would read them on study breaks, hunched in her favorite carrel in the library. In one short, somber letter, George told Donna that the sergeant who had handed him Donna's first letter at Christmas had been killed by sniper fire. He had been engaged.

Once, when she heard on the news that a marine from Boston had been killed, she gasped, "Oh my God!" George was from Boston, and she thought—Please, let it not be *my* George. Later, she found out that it wasn't him.

For eighteen months, Donna and George exchanged letters, building a friendship out of words alone.

In the spring of 1985, Donna was preparing to graduate from the University of Akron. She had landed a job with a computer company in Columbus, Ohio, and right after graduation she and her cousin Diane decided to have one more fling with freedom before Donna started work. They picked Myrtle Beach, a buzzing vacation spot in South Carolina.

Donna and Diane planned to drive the fifteen hours from Hartford to Myrtle Beach. As Donna plotted their route on a map, a realization hit her. "We're going to be driving through North Carolina," Donna told Diane.

"So?" Diane said.

"George is stationed there—at Camp Le Jeune. We'll be passing right by it. He's been there ever since he got back from Beirut. We're still exchanging letters. I've never actually met him. Hey—" Donna said, becoming excited by the idea. "Why don't we stop there on the way to Myrtle Beach? I'd like to meet him."

Donna called George at Camp Le Jeune; it was the first time they had spoken over the phone. George had a Boston accent and he sounded nervous.

"It will be great to finally meet you," he said, feeling his knees go weak.

George asked his friend John to join them so he could escort Donna's cousin if they all went out.

"Okay, I'll do it," John agreed. Then he added, "But you owe me one."

Camp Le Jeune was a huge military base populated mostly by young male soldiers—so when Donna and Diane arrived one sunny afternoon in their brown Camaro, they received a great deal of attention. The arrival of a civilian woman was always an occasion, but the vision of two beautiful, college girls stopping by on their way to a beach resort was almost too much. The military police officer who admitted them at the front gate stared longingly after them as they drove in, and as they cruised through camp looking for George's barracks, marines hollered and cheered and fell all over themselves trying to get their attention.

"You'd think they had never seen a woman before," Diane remarked.

When they reached the right barracks, they had to wait as the marine on duty called George. Donna felt anxious. After a few minutes, George emerged. He sported a military haircut so short that on first glance Donna thought he was bald. He had the muscles of a bodybuilder and a simple tattoo on his right bicep—USMC. Both girls noticed his piercing blue eyes. Looking at Donna, his mouth fell open. She stepped forward and hugged him.

"It's me," she said. "Donna."

"How was your trip?" George asked, his heart beating like a drum.

That evening, the four of them went to town for a candlelit dinner. John was in high spirits after meeting Diane. George brought flowers and was exceedingly polite and gracious: an old-fashioned gentleman. At first, it was an effort for George to make conversation—he was so shy. Donna was even lovelier than he had imagined from her letters and the one high school photo she had sent.

George was unlike the men Donna was accustomed to going out with. His marked politeness and sincerity gave Donna the impression that he did not view dating as a casual pastime. Irish-Catholic, George had grown up in the working-class section of Woburn, just north of Boston. He was serious and hard-working, the oldest of five children in a family that had seen difficult times. As a child he had taken his earnings from bagging groceries at the local market home to his mother, and his younger brothers and sister had always looked up to him.

George paid for dinner, and he insisted on paying for Donna and Diane's hotel room. The next morning, he arrived with balloons to see them off. Donna hugged him good-bye, and she was struck by the kindness in his eyes. As they drove away, Donna felt suddenly despondent, thinking she might never see him again.

At Myrtle Beach, the girls checked in to one of the many hotels along the beach. Later that day, the clerk phoned their room: Two men were waiting for them in lobby. In the elevator, Diane said, "It's got to be your marine."

Corporal George McLean and Corporal John Bird stood stiffly near the registration desk.

"George!" Donna exclaimed. "How on earth did you find us?"

The marines had obtained ninety-six-hour passes that morning and then scoured the coast, inquiring at hotel after hotel until they finally found them. Because it was tourist season, not a single empty room was available on the whole beach. The guys slept on the balcony and paid for the girls' meals and hotel bill.

Donna and George spent the next three days deepening their friendship—which had begun a year and a half earlier with a letter cast aloft like a prayer. They took long walks on the beach and lingered over sunset dinners. On one walk, George stopped and turned to Donna, gently clasping her shoulders and kissing her.

"I know we're going to be married," he said.

His certainty took Donna by surprise. He talked about marriage and children, and Donna fell under the spell of his convictions. She had never met a man with a more admirable character, so strong and devoted. After Myrtle Beach, Donna and George's relationship became exclusive. They still wrote—Donna from Columbus and George from Camp Le Jeune—but their letters took a romantic turn. They dated long-distance for two years and then became engaged before they ever lived in the same city. They married in 1988 and now live with their two children in Ohio.

They keep all the letters and cards they exchanged in a special box. They had both, without the other knowing, saved and guarded each one.

The Portrait

~

*H*ERBERT BEGAN TO paint when he was a child growing up in Hungary in the 1930s. Over time he refined his brush strokes and became adept at using vibrant colors. At first, he painted everything around him—his mother's china and ceramic vases, the living room furniture, city landscapes. But as he grew older, he developed a talent for portraiture. Even at a young age, he was able to capture the depth and poignancy of the human countenance on canvas.

The outbreak of World War II put Herbert's painting on hold—just as it suspended all normal life in Europe. Like countless others, Herbert was caught in the snare of the Nazi death machine. Everyone in his family was sent to Auschwitz, one of Poland's most notorious death camps. Tall and fair at the age of fourteen, he passed for older and was allowed to work rather than be put to immediate death. In this way he escaped the fate of his four younger brothers.

The war took Herbert's entire family; he was the only survivor. When it ended, he was sent to one of the refugee camps set up by the American government in cities across Europe. For the next few years, such camps were home to tens of thousands of war victims: people recovered from the war, searched for lost relatives and friends, and waited until they could find a permanent home. The youngest and more resilient survivors started new families and made new friends. In fact, record numbers of marriages and births took place in the refugee centers in the years following the war.

Herbert was charismatic, quick-witted, and quite popular. A kind American soldier took a liking to him, and Herbert eventually felt close enough to ask, "Can I get some paper and a pencil? I used to draw."

"I'll see what I can do," the American replied. A few days later, the soldier handed Herbert a package. Herbert held it close to his chest and found a quiet place to unwrap its contents. He carefully removed one sheet of paper and the pencil. He took his time flattening the sheet's creases. Then he slowly reached for the pencil, took it between his fingers, and savored the smell of lead.

Using shadows, light blacks, and grays, Herbert composed amazingly expressive portraits of the faces around him, always with a sadness about the eyes.

Herbert befriended a girl his age named Doti. She had lost everyone in her family except her sister, Elsa, who had relocated to England after the war. After learning that Doti was still alive and living in a refugee center in Germany, Elsa sent Doti a black-and-white photo of herself.

One afternoon when Doti and Herbert were together, Doti showed him the photo.

"Please, Herbert, can you paint this?" Doti asked. "This is

my sister, Elsa. She's in England. It is small, but perhaps you can draw a larger one."

Herbert held the tiny black-and-white print. Staring back at him was a remarkably beautiful teenage girl, fair-haired like himself.

"I'll do it right away," he answered. He looked at Doti. "I promise to be careful with the photograph."

For the next few days Herbert occupied himself drawing Elsa's portrait. He did not want to capture just her obvious beauty, but all her life's tribulations. When he was done, her expression was a bit haunting and aged beneath a brave, tender smile, an expression not unlike his own.

Herbert spent two years at the refugee camp before immigrating to New York City. In New York, he was stricken with a bout of tuberculosis, which he had contracted during the war. His doctors recommended he move to Denver, Colorado, where the air was healthier and there were hospitals that specialized in the disease. So Herbert moved west. He recovered and continued to paint. He won a scholarship to a fine arts school in Denver, where he made his new home.

Meanwhile, Doti's sister, Elsa, spent several more years in England and then immigrated to New York City. There, she also tested positive for tuberculosis, and doctors advised her to move to Colorado, which she did. Once in Denver, she went for another tuberculosis test.

"The results are negative," her doctor informed her. Elsa was confused. "It's good news," the doctor added. "You don't have tuberculosis." Elsa, having never seen a place so beautiful, decided to stay in Denver anyway.

In cities all across the United States, the Europeans who immigrated there after the war often got together, forming substitute families that lasted for lifetimes. Denver was no exception. One evening Herbert attended a celebration at the home of a friend.

As usual, Herbert's wit and charm attracted a small circle of friends. As he chatted happily, a break in the circle revealed a lovely blond girl a few feet away. Herbert got up and stood off to the side, quietly watching the woman bewitch the other young gentlemen with her gentle, attractive smile. After a few minutes, he approached her.

"I recognize you," he said, studying her.

She shook her head; she had never seen him before. Her placid eyes seemed to smile up at him. As he studied her face, he suddenly flashed back to the tiny black-and-white photo. It was Elsa!

"I painted your portrait!" he exclaimed, triumphant. "Your sister, she gave me a picture of you years ago—in Germany!" Herbert shook his head in disbelief. "I painted your portrait from the photograph," he said, adding, "this is rather remarkable."

"I sent my sister a picture I had taken after the war," Elsa said. "That must be the one you painted. Doti never mentioned it to me."

SO BEGAN Herbert and Elsa's life together. They married in 1953, soon after that first meeting, and raised one daughter. Sadly, Elsa's portrait was lost in the move from Europe to the United States and its whereabouts is still unknown.

The Play's the Thing

⌒

JENNIFER WAS A theater arts major at Loyola Marymount College. Petite, with thin, narrow hips, a girlish face, slightly freckled skin, and baby-fine hair, Jennifer was regularly cast in the role of the ingenue. While this part was often a leading role, Jennifer was a serious and talented student who, by her senior year, was beginning to chafe at playing the role of the spirited, naïve, female character.

In one acting class during Jennifer's senior year, her drama professor decided to produce *The Three Sisters* by the famous Russian playwright Anton Chekhov. Jennifer's professor knew her well and took her aside before the parts were assigned.

"I think you'd be perfect as Irena," she said. "The part's yours."

Jennifer sighed. Irena was gentle, dreamy, and the youngest of the three sisters.

"I really would rather play Masha," Jennifer said.

"Oh? I thought you would be thrilled."

"I feel much more like Masha than Irena these days," Jennifer said. Masha was the second of the sisters. She was stuck in an unhappy marriage to a kind but unremarkable man. Though her drama teacher was surprised at her request, she agreed to cast Jennifer as Masha.

Jennifer had been seeing her boyfriend, Kevin, for four years. He was kind, solid, and he genuinely loved her—and Jennifer loved him. But their relationship was growing stale, their conversations dull. He preferred soccer, while she pursued the theater. She felt it was time for them to decide whether to get married or not, but she feared falling into marriage simply because they'd been together for so long. Could they reinvigorate their relationship—or would it always be like this, tepid and unexciting?

Meeting Matthew confused her even more. Five years older than everyone else, with pale, thoughtful eyes and strawberry blond hair, Matthew was in two of her drama classes. He was sophisticated and worldly: After high school, he had traveled the globe performing with a singing group, and he had just returned from studying drama in London. He had taken other drama courses at Loyola over the years, but he and Jennifer hadn't met before, though their paths must have crossed many times. Now they seemed to bump into each other constantly— in class, in the bookstore, in line for senior photos.

In class, Jennifer found Matthew's observations about acting and plays to be analytical, thoughtful, and incisive. One afternoon, when there were not enough scripts to go around, Matthew and Jennifer shared one. She was nervous sitting beside him, and she was unusually shy around Matthew whenever they did acting exercises together. Jennifer realized she found him increasingly attractive.

Their drama professor continued casting the roles for *The Three Sisters*.

"Matthew," she said, "you'll be playing the role of Colonel Vershinin."

Jennifer felt her face flush. In the play, Vershinin is the dashing colonel who arrives suddenly at the sisters' country house. In time, he becomes Masha's lover.

Jennifer began to prepare for the play. One afternoon, she stood in front of the mirror, alone, practicing her lines from an early scene. When Masha first appears, she is bewailing the dullness of her marriage.

"I'm bored, bored, bored!" Jennifer read from the script. Then she stopped. That's me, she thought. Bored—with Kevin. To sort out her feelings, she began to jot them down in a diary.

Jennifer and Matthew also began to rehearse their scenes together, both in and out of class. They had spirited conversations about *The Three Sisters*, sharing their love of theater and literature. In time, their conversations became more personal.

I'm beginning to feel guilty when I'm with Matthew, she wrote in her diary.

One afternoon, Jennifer and Matthew got together to rehearse the scene where Masha and Vershinin confess their frustrations with their marriages. But instead of practicing, Matthew and Jennifer started talking about their own lives. Jennifer confided in Matthew her feelings about her situation with her boyfriend. Matthew listened, empathetic.

He said, "I was also in a four-year relationship. We kept trying to make it work, but nothing seemed to help. We just became unhappy."

They talked so long they never got around to practicing the scene; the first time they practiced it was in class. The actors took their places and the class turned their attention to the front of the room. Matthew glanced at his script, then dropped it to his side:

As Vershinin sits in the sisters' parlor room, Masha tells him how unhappy she is with her husband. Then Vershinin unburdens himself.

"Why are the [Russian's] aspirations so low? Why is he so fed up with his wife?"

"Why indeed?" Masha replies.

"Why is his wife fed up with him? You should have seen her today, what a squalid creature she is. We started squabbling at seven o'clock this morning and at nine o'clock I walked out and slammed the door."

Vershinin looks at Masha, his voice softer. "I never talk about it normally. You're the only one I ever complain to." Vershinin kisses her hand.

Later that night, Jennifer wrote in her diary about how remarkably her earlier conversations with Matthew mirrored the scene in the play.

Jennifer and Matthew grew closer. One afternoon after class, he told her, "I remember watching you in a play a couple of years ago."

"Really? Which one?"

"What the Butler Saw."

Jennifer smiled. "It's funny. I don't remember ever seeing you before this class," she said.

"Oh, I was around. When I saw you in the play, I thought, Wow, she's hot."

As showtime for *The Three Sisters* drew nearer, the class assembled for the final run-through. Until now, Jennifer had managed to avoid kissing Matthew in the scene where Vershinin confesses his unhappy marriage. Once, when the bell rang a moment before the kiss, Jennifer exclaimed, "Oh that's the bell! I've got to run!" Jennifer later berated herself: *I'm acting like a total baby,* she wrote in her diary. But she still felt loyal to Kevin despite her strong attraction to Matthew.

The morning of the dress rehearsal, Jennifer jumped out of bed. She was excited and nervous, knowing she could no longer avoid the kiss at the end of the scene. And she realized that Masha's love for Colonel Vershinin mirrored her own feelings for Matthew.

In class, excitement electrified the room. The actors, in costume, took their places. Those not on stage intently watched the performance. One by one, the characters re-created life in the Russian countryside on the cusp of the Revolution:

The arrival of Vershinin, a colonel in the czar's army and on his way to crush the rebellion, turns the three sisters' lives upside down. An attraction between Masha and Vershinin begins to develop as soon as they meet. Olia, the eldest sister, disapproves, but Masha is too unhappy in her marriage to care.

In act II, scene I, Matthew and Jennifer claimed the stage. All eyes fell on them. The chemistry between them was palpable:

After confiding in each other about their unhappy marriages, Vershinin and Masha draw closer. He gently cradles her face in his hands.

"I'm in love with your eyes, with the way you move. I dream about it," Vershinin says. "You are a magnificent, magical woman."

"When you talk to me like that, I don't know why, but I find myself laughing. Even though it frightens me," Masha replies. Vershinin kisses her and Masha does not resist.

"I'm in love, I'm in love!" Vershinin cries.

"Don't do that again!" Masha implores. Vershinin kisses her again. "Or rather do," she says. An abrupt knock on the door stops them.

Jennifer's heart beat quickly and her face was hot. Their kiss was so genuine and passionate she could not be sure whether it was Matthew or Vershinin who had kissed her.

After the dress rehearsal, Jennifer knew she had to break things off with Kevin. She could never marry him. That afternoon, she ended their long-standing relationship; it was easier than she had imagined it would be.

That night, the cast of *The Three Sisters* celebrated the successful dress rehearsal at a Russian restaurant. Feeling tipsy after a few drinks, Jennifer went up to Matthew and gave him a hard kiss. They danced all evening until Matthew drove her home.

Soon afterward, Matthew invited Jennifer to watch a production of *The Three Sisters* at a nearby theater, and from then on they saw each other exclusively. After dating for two years, they married in 1996. They still share a passion for theater, acting in and producing plays. And now Matthew and Jennifer are also raising a family.

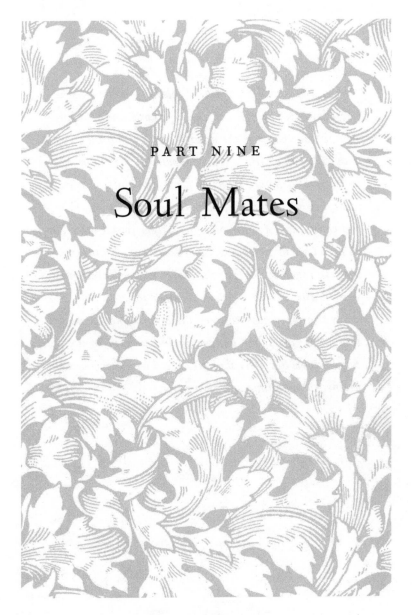

PART NINE

Soul Mates

IT *is always wonderful to hear tales of magic—stories where love appears like a bolt of lightning, and both partners get together with the inner assurance that they have found the "One". But such an experience is not the only, nor even the defining, aspect of being soul mates. Commitment through hard times, shared joys and passions, faith, dedication, and a willingness to sacrifice for the other are all hallmarks of soul mates. Sometimes that sense of knowing assurance in our partner only develops over many years—after we have grown together through time and many trials and have suffered through the prosaic doubts that are a part of the human condition. In these stories, couples come to believe they are indeed with their intended partner through time and experience.*

For Better or for Worse

~⁓~

*I*N 1985, WHEN she was twenty-one, Alison became a hairdresser. She graduated near the top of her class in cosmetology school and worked long days in a busy shop in a small, blue-collar town in eastern Ohio. Women came to the salon as much to exchange gossip and catch up with acquaintances as to get a cut and a style. Somewhere between the rinse and the chair, talk would begin about children, the weather, or wayward husbands as the client relaxed under the skilled hands of the hairdresser.

Five feet tall, petite, dark-haired, and fiery, Alison talked a good deal herself, quickly, as if to get it all in. She moved energetically with her comb and scissors, deftly transforming limp, styleless hair into something beautiful—all the while maintaining a spirited discussion about her close-knit Italian family, the newest hair product, or the dates she went on, a couple of which were with steel-mill workers from the next town.

One of the hairdressers at Alison's salon also cut men's hair. Scott, a twenty-eight-year-old welder, came about every three months to get his hair cut. Scott liked to watch Alison from across the room, sometimes catching portions of her conversations. When she caught him looking, she would smile warmly and he would half lower his head and smile shyly back, wholly unaware of the dashing figure he cut: six-foot-four with startlingly green eyes.

Scott started coming in for haircuts more often—every two months, then every six weeks. Soon it was once a month. The few times when Alison wasn't busy with a customer, he tried to make small talk with her. Alison's fellow stylists would simply nod knowingly at one another whenever Scott arrived, his hair in perfect shape, for another trim. Soon he was coming every three weeks.

After about eight months, the phone rang at the shop—it was for Alison. She listened for a moment and then said, "Sure." After she hung up, she turned to everyone in the salon. "It was Scott," she announced. "He finally asked me out." A few of the hairdressers cheered.

Scott, hounded by a friend to make the call, invited Alison to a popular restaurant and bar in a nearby town. On the day of their date, the weather service issued a tornado warning. Before noon, thick, gray clouds darkened the sky, and it was hot and muggy—and it was only May. Later, in the early evening, as Alison worked on her last client, an eerie silence blanketed the town. There was not a single gust of wind, not a drop of rain, not a bird to be heard or seen anywhere.

"Strangest weather I've ever seen," someone in the salon said. A little later, hail the size of baseballs plunged from the sky. Everyone ran to the front of the shop to look: They had never seen anything like it. After about a half an hour it stopped, and

Alison quietly packed her things and left to get ready for her date. She was not superstitious, but the storm did not seem to be a good sign.

Scott picked her up in his truck and they drove to the restaurant. By then, thirty-mile-an-hour gusts blew heavy rain in all directions. They drove in silence listening to news on the radio. The tornado had hit a nearby town of about eight hundred, practically leveling it. Alison shivered in her seat.

"Oh, this is just awful," she cried. She crossed her arms tightly to her chest; she felt like she was coming down with something herself. When they reached the restaurant, Scott held an umbrella over her head as they dashed inside.

The restaurant was crowded with people who had stopped to get out of the rain. Everyone was talking about the tornado. Scott and Alison shook beads of water from their clothes as they took their seats at a table. A waitress came over and handed them a couple of menus. "The report just came in. About fifteen people died in Niles," she informed them. Alison put her hand to her mouth and Scott shook his head slowly from side to side.

"Oh my God!" Alison cried.

"They said the town was flattened. Everything but the steel mill," she said matter-of-factly.

"The mill didn't get hit?" Scott asked.

"Strangest thing. Not a scratch." The mill supported hundreds of families in the surrounding towns.

Despite the tornado, Scott and Alison got along uncommonly well on their first date. Scott was relaxed, kind, and easy to be with; his mellow qualities seemed to complement her more fiery and effusive personality. By the end of their second date a few days later, Scott and Alison both sensed something right about their relationship.

About a week later, Scott asked her out again. Alison begged off, saying that she thought she was on the verge of getting a cold. Soon after, he asked her out again, but she still declined.

"You're gonna think I'm crazy," she said. "But I think I'm coming down with the flu again. I wouldn't want to infect you or anything. I'm sure I'll be better in a couple of days." At work, she felt tired. At the end of a long day, she had to sit down and rest a few minutes before she had enough energy to drive home. Alison called her doctor. He said that she had been working too hard and to take a few days off. "People your age run around too much," he told her.

She and Scott continued to see each other, and after a short break, she returned to work—but she wasn't feeling any better. After about a month, Scott noticed a lump on Alison's neck. She made an appointment to see her doctor the next Friday.

"It's probably just a swollen thyroid gland," Scott said reassuringly.

A surgeon took a biopsy of the lump. Scott waited with her for the results; she thought it better not to mention anything to her family in case it was nothing. A while later, the nurse showed them into the doctor's office.

"I'm going to be straight with you," the doctor said. "You have cancer."

Alison felt her heart drop. Scott looked over at her with concern.

"There are hundreds of little tumors in the specimen we

took of your lymph node," the doctor continued. "The cancer looks aggressive."

Not quite believing what she was hearing, Alison said nothing.

The doctor went on. "Now I don't know how bad it is. I have no way of knowing that. You'll need more tests so we can get a better idea. We'll set you up to see an oncologist as soon as possible."

"Are you sure those are *my* test results?" she asked.

"I'm sure," he said. "I wish I wasn't."

They can't be talking about me, Alison thought, sitting silently, paralyzed, while Scott asked the doctor some more questions. As they got up to leave, the surgeon pulled Scott aside and thanked him for being there.

"I wouldn't have wanted to tell her if you hadn't been here for her," the doctor said.

When Scott and Alison were alone, he said to her, "We'll get through this."

Out of four stages of lymphoma, Alison was diagnosed with stage three. Extensive testing revealed that tumors had spread to her stomach. The oncologist and surgeon agreed that her lymph nodes and spleen would have to be removed. Then they planned to treat the rest of her organs with large doses of radiation. If she survived the cancer, she would still not be the same. Without a spleen, she would have impaired immunity. A common cold could be deadly. The radiation would damage her organs in ways that they could not accurately predict. And she might never have children.

"Oh, I'm going to lose my hair!" she cried. The thought of that seemed to bother her more than anything else.

"I will love you bald," he replied.

"How can you say that!" she snapped. "I'm a hairdresser!"

The evening before her first surgery, Scott sat with Alison. She had been crying for days. In a quiet moment she looked at him. Her face stiffened in a serious expression: An inner strength seemed to suddenly surface.

"There's nothing holding you here," she said without emotion. "You're free to leave." He looked at her incredulously. "Now's the time to go," she said in the same flat tone. She had been sick ever since she had known him without either of them realizing it. She didn't want to put him through what was about to happen. After all, they hadn't been dating long before her diagnosis, and it wasn't his burden.

"Don't be dumb," he answered. Neither of them mentioned it again.

Scott stayed by Alison's side through the painful surgeries and the agonizing radiation treatments. He never once considered leaving, even when she wept with pain and complained angrily for days on end. She barked at any suggestion to make her more comfortable. "This is not making me feel better," she would snap. "This treatment is worse than the disease." The radiation burned her tongue and throat, making it impossible for her to eat. She would wretch violently and break out into fits of crying. She had never been more miserable.

When her throat healed some, Scott brought her her favorite Subway sandwich and lifted the shades.

"Look, it's beautiful outside," he said.

"I can't eat this—can't you see I'm sick!" she cried. "Nothing you can bring or nothing you can say is going to make me feel better."

Scott never lost heart. He always met her frowns with a smile and reacted to her angry words with kind ones. Toward the end of her radiation treatment, when she was feeling better, Scott would, again, bring her favorite sandwich, with another favorite treat: Dairy Queen ice cream, plain vanilla.

When Scott was leaving after one particular hospital visit, Alison blew him a kiss.

"You're my angel," she said softly.

The radiation and surgeries successfully wiped out Alison's cancer. But the doctors told her there was a good chance it could recur later in life and that she faced other lifelong complications. At the end of her treatment, in December 1985, she and Scott became engaged; they married a year later.

IN 1988, Alison became pregnant. None of her doctors could understand how she had conceived, since during her radiation treatment, her ovaries had been tied to the back of her uterus to prevent damage and were never untied. "We're just doctors, not God," one told her.

Today, Scott still works as a welder; Alison now works in the medical profession. They live with their son on the East Coast. Alison's cancer remains in remission.

American Sports Fans

⌐

*N*ANCY BECAME A sports fan in a town where being a "fan" is taken very seriously. In Boston, where Nancy was born and raised, true fans follow all the local teams and know every player, every victory, every playoff game. They know all the statistics and the lore with devotional intensity. In baseball, it is the ill-fated Boston Red Sox; in hockey, the roughneck Boston Bruins; and in basketball, the mightiest of them all, the championship Boston Celtics.

A tomboy as a child, Nancy grew up in a family of avid athletes and spectators. She knew the rules of football and basketball before she even knew what it meant to kiss a boy. Slim and lithe, with girl-next-door looks, she had a perpetual tan from playing outdoors with her two older brothers.

She never even dated until college. She attended Emory University in Atlanta, Georgia, where she was still more interested in sports than boys. After graduation, she stayed in Atlanta for a number of years, but after her family relocated to Del Rey Beach, Florida, she decided to move down there, too, in 1985, to be closer to them. Wherever Nancy was, she always rooted for her hometown teams, especially the Celtics.

In Del Rey Beach, Nancy moved into a sprawling apartment complex, complete with swimming pool, Jacuzzi, tennis courts, and a gym. At twenty-seven, Nancy worked as a controller for a computer company.

Bill also lived in Nancy's apartment building. Twenty-four years old, Bill was friendly, garrulous, large, and almost bearlike in appearance. He was such an avid sports fan that his grandmother often remarked, "Bill, you had better marry a girl who likes sports."

He had recently moved to Florida from California to help a friend start a computer business. However, once his friend's business was up and running, he planned to return to California. For ten months, Bill and Nancy lived five doors from each other on the second floor, but they never met. Nancy always used the nearby elevator. Bill always took the stairs.

One Tuesday evening, Bill sat in the Jacuzzi, his head still buzzing from the spectacular playoff victory that afternoon by his favorite basketball team, the Los Angeles Lakers. That win had earned them the right to play their archrival, the Boston Celtics, for the NBA championship, which would begin next week.

Just then, Nancy and a male friend headed toward the Jacuzzi. It turned out that Bill knew the friend.

Reveling in the Lakers' victory, Bill asked his friend if he had seen the game.

"Yeah, I caught the second half."

Nancy and her friend settled into the Jacuzzi as Bill continued passionately. "The Lakers are going to do it this time. This is our year. It will be great to finally get the monkey off our back." The Lakers had not beaten the Celtics for years and for that alone he despised the Boston team.

Nancy replied knowingly, "No way. It will be the Celtics as usual. You can't beat Larry Bird."

"We'll see," Bill answered, conceding nothing.

Nancy and Bill continued to discuss basketball, dissecting the previous season and exchanging opinions on the merits of various players and teams—while their friend seemed to vanish into the bubbles of the Jacuzzi. Nancy knew the outcomes of every season going back more than a decade. She was merely displaying the knowledge of any true Boston sports aficionado—but Bill was impressed. So much so that he even forgave her for being a Celtics fan. Of course, Bill also noticed Nancy's trim physique and sunny disposition. Then, suddenly, he felt an overwhelming compulsion—he still doesn't know why—to test her knowledge in another sport.

"When did the New York Jets win the Super Bowl?" Bill asked abruptly. Before Nancy could respond, Bill answered his own question. "It was 1970."

"No," Nancy corrected him. "It was 1969. Joe Namath carried the game."

She was right. It was 1969. That was the moment Bill's grandmother had foretold: This was the girl for him.

A few days later, Bill decided to invite Nancy to watch the first game of the NBA championships with him on the big-screen television in the clubhouse. Since the Celtics were playing, he was pretty sure she wouldn't refuse. He would bring the beer and pizza.

He walked five doors down the hall and rang the bell.

Nancy had just hopped out of the shower. She was expecting a girlfriend to arrive any minute, so she flung open the door with a towel wrapped around her head and another around her body.

"Can I borrow a towel?" Bill asked, without missing a beat.

Nancy turned a deep shade of red and scurried behind the door.

"Just a minute," she called out. "I'll be ready in a minute." Then she shut the door on him.

Nancy's friend arrived moments later, and she sensed that she had walked into the middle of something. Bill was standing patiently in the hall, a delighted grin on his face, happy to wait for Nancy in front of the now closed door.

BILL AND Nancy watched the first game of the 1985 playoffs together—and the next two after that. They each passionately rooted for their home teams. Then Nancy had to fly to Philadelphia for a family event. Her return flight was scheduled during the final game, which meant she'd miss seeing who prevailed for the season's top honors. Bill called from Florida and offered to pick her up from the airport; he promised to buy champagne and flowers if the Lakers won. Nancy accepted, not the least bit offended by Bill's stipulation. After all, the Lakers were his team.

On the plane en route to Miami, Nancy could only speculate how the game was turning out. Then, when they landed, the copilot announced over the loudspeaker that the Lakers had won the championship. Cheers rose from some of the passengers.

When Nancy entered the terminal, Bill was waiting for her with a huge grin on his face. As promised, champagne and flowers were waiting in the car. For the first time in Nancy's life, a Celtics loss didn't upset her. She was just happy to see Bill, brawny and smiling and so obviously happy to see her.

After six months, they became engaged. They now live in California, where they are raising another generation of American sports fans.

Carolina Chooses

CAROLINA RODE HER bike home as fast as she could. Her heart raced as she prayed, her eyes closed: Please let this be an acceptance this time. She jumped off her bike, letting it fall to the ground, and ran into the house. The envelope lay on the kitchen table.

Carolina picked up the letter. Her face was flushed and her heart was beating so fast she could barely breathe. She tore the envelope open and unfolded the letter—her eyes could barely focus. With the first words, "We regret to inform you," Carolina cried out. Her mother came into the room and put her arms around her daughter's shoulders.

Carolina burst into tears. "Oh it's impossible! I'll never get in!"

Ever since she could remember, Carolina wanted to be a doctor. She lived in a small village in Sweden and had been brought up by a close, loving family. Carolina had worked extremely hard in school, her head buried in her books most of the time, but it was very difficult to get in to any of the country's few medical schools. Her only other passion was gymnastics, which she pursued with the same intensity; she had won several youth championship titles in Sweden. Carolina was graceful with straight, blond hair and light blue eyes—a natural beauty.

Over the next few years while Carolina worked as a nurse, she continued submitting yearly applications to medical school. She was now twenty-five, and for the last seven years she had been going out with a handsome Swede named Erik. He was a mirror of herself—tall, intelligent, ambitious—and all of her friends seemed to agree, "Oh, they will get married, those two."

Carolina ignored their remarks. She knew she would never marry him, but could not say why. She knew in the same way that at nine years old she had known her family was in danger as they drove to the mountains for a ski trip. They had been on the road for almost four hours when Carolina, sitting in the back of the car, panicked. She demanded that her father stop the car and that everyone put on seatbelts.

"But we're only ten minutes away. Why stop now?" her mother said.

"We must stop the car!" Carolina shouted.

"Carolina!" her mother scolded. But Carolina was inconsolable.

"All right," her mother relented. "We'll put on our seatbelts." She looked at Carolina, who had calmed down, and shook her head. They resumed driving. Two minutes later, the car's steering mechanism malfunctioned, her father lost control, and the car skidded and flipped over. No one was seriously injured because they were all belted in.

One afternoon, after Carolina had recently completed yet another medical school application, she got together with her two best friends. Still immersed with thoughts of what would happen with her application, she barely listened to their excited chatter.

"Come with us to America," they said. "We're going to California. It's near the beach! You can have your own room."

"I don't know," she said.

"Is it because of Erik?"

"No, it's not Erik."

"Come on. You can't keep applying to medical school your whole life. This is a perfect opportunity."

"I'll think about it," she said. But there wasn't much to decide. Not long afterward she agreed to meet her friends in Los Angeles, California.

After Carolina arrived, she got a job with a catering company, and in a couple of months she was dating the owner— even though she knew instinctively she would never marry him, either.

After a year in California, Carolina jumped at an offer to teach gymnastics. Early that summer, she arranged a gymnastics competition. Three of the participants were a set of triplets. While their parents snapped photos, Ron, a family friend and the triplets' karate instructor, videotaped their performance.

At one point Carolina glanced over at Ron. As she looked at him, a strange sensation swept over her. His eyes met hers. A moment later, she looked away; his presence agitated her. She focused again on the competition, peering at Ron now and then. He had dark, curly hair cropped close to his head and strong, masculine features. He was muscular and well-built, but he moved easily, as if he were weightless.

Two months later, while leafing through a local weekly

paper, a friend of Carolina's suggested that they take a karate class together.

"I don't think so," Carolina said. "I prefer gymnastics."

"Come on. It's something new to try."

"I know I won't like it."

"How can you be so stubborn? You won't know until you've tried it." They went back and forth, until finally Carolina yielded.

But Carolina didn't like it. She felt awkward and intimidated during class. She was so distracted by her efforts that she didn't even notice Ron was in the room.

At thirty-two, Ron ran his own a karate school, or dojo. He was introduced to karate at fourteen, growing up in Israel. All through school he practiced three hours a day. When he turned twenty, he moved to California to follow his Japanese karate master who ran a famous dojo there.

This karate master, well into his seventies, was still considered the world's greatest. Ron studied at his dojo for one year before the old master even noticed him; then he took Ron under his wing. The master helped Ron hone his skills, preparing him for world competition. Ron went on to win several world championships, and eventually his mentor handpicked him to become one of the world's next great karate masters.

Even though she hated it at first, Carolina agreed to try karate one more time. She felt suddenly determined to master her fear of learning something new. The second time back, she noticed Ron, who was working one-on-one with a student, and the effect was explosive—she *had* to talk to him. Toward the end of class, as the room emptied out, she inched her way closer to him. A woman—Ron's girlfriend of two years—stood beside him. Ron looked up as Carolina approached.

"Did you like the class?" he asked her, speaking in a forward manner.

Ron was the shy, silent type. Carolina couldn't have guessed that it was unusual for him to speak out that way.

"Yes. Better than last time," she mumbled.

"It gets better with practice," he said reassuringly.

Ron's girlfriend crept closer to Ron until she was almost touching him.

"I'd like to sign up—" Carolina was having difficulty focusing her eyes whenever she looked at Ron. She felt foolish. Ron, blushing a little, muttered something about a schedule. Ron's girlfriend turned to him and abruptly reminded him that her brother was coming from Canada next week to stay at their place.

"Oh, right," Ron said distractedly.

His girlfriend glared at Carolina and said, "Let's go, Ron," pulling him by the arm. But before they could leave, Carolina bolted from the studio. Ron turned to watch her go.

Outside, Carolina nervously unlocked the chain from her bike and got on. She rode home, tears streaming down her cheeks. She didn't even notice that it had started to rain.

As she cried, she suddenly knew with mysterious certainty that she was meant to marry this man. If I don't marry him, she thought, I will never marry at all. In her distress she didn't notice Ron, who was following her at a distance to make sure she arrived home safely in the rain.

Carolina did not go back to class. She was living with the

caterer, whom she'd been seeing for a year and a half, and she didn't know what to do about her strong feelings for Ron. He was dating someone, too, and Carolina was hesitant to see him again. After a few days, Ron called her.

"I haven't seen you in class," he said.

Carolina was so relieved to hear from him, she simply asked, "Is it too late to sign up?"

Carolina began studying karate under Ron, and she soon became quite competent. In the meantime, Ron broke up with his girlfriend.

One day after class, Ron invited Carolina to attend a traditional ceremony to honor the beginning students who had earned their yellow belts.

"Why don't you come with me?" he asked.

Carolina smiled. "I'd love to."

When Carolina told her boyfriend she planned to go to a karate ceremony that night—kissing him lightly on the cheek as she left—he sensed that something between them had changed irreparably.

After the ceremony, Ron asked Carolina to have dinner with him that night. They ate at a Japanese restaurant and talked until three in the morning. Afterward, as they walked to Ron's car, he put his arm around her.

"I know we are going to get married," he said.

Carolina nodded; she knew it, too. They sat in silence as he drove her home.

After that night, Carolina was in high spirits. Two days later, her mother called from Sweden.

"Carolina!" she cried. "You've been accepted to medical school!"

Carolina put the receiver to her chest. She could hear her mother shouting, "Carolina! Carolina!" But she could barely think.

"I'll call you back," she said, her thoughts spinning. School started in two weeks. If she wanted to do it, she would have to leave right away. And yet how could she do that now? It was an impossible choice. But over and over in her head she kept thinking incredulously, "I got in. I got in."

She called her mom back. "Please enroll me. I'll be coming home in two weeks."

Then she broke the news to Ron.

"I've worked my whole life for this," she told him. "I could never forgive myself if I didn't at least give it a try." To herself, she thought, fate brought us together once. I have to trust it will happen again.

After Carolina had been back in Sweden only two weeks, Ron came to visit. A few months later, Ron was in Europe teaching karate. On his way home, he stopped in Sweden to see Carolina and spend Christmas vacation with her and her family.

"Come home with me," he said before he left.

"I can't," she said.

But over the next couple of months, Ron's absence felt like a physical pain. My life is with him, she thought. I'm sure of it.

The following February, she left medical school for good and flew to California. A few months later, Carolina and Ron married. Today, they have two children, and Ron runs a popular karate school where Carolina teaches gymnastics.

Best Friends

⌒

$\mathcal{F}$RIENDS WHO HEAR about Mark and Lindy's engagement often remark, "You grew up in the same city, but had to travel halfway across the world to meet." And it's true. Mark and Lindy both grew up in an enclave of Durban, a city on the coast of South Africa with stately homes and groomed lawns. They both attended the same preschool, the same elementary school, and the same high school. Their grandparents were good friends, and their parents were acquaintances who ran in the same social circles. Though Mark is three years older than Lindy, they must have crossed paths a hundred times. Still, they never met. But perhaps a prior meeting wouldn't have mattered, because when they finally did meet in Los Angeles as young adults Mark had no romantic intentions toward Lindy. Instead, they became best friends.

While still in South Africa, Lindy earned a bachelor's degree in public relations and moved to Cape Town, where she worked for a PR firm for several years. In 1993, she decided to travel the globe for a year. Midway through her travels, she stopped in Los Angeles and stayed with a friend who lived in Santa Monica. Part glamour, part funk, Santa Monica reminded Lindy of Durban. She liked it so much that she decided to look for a job there, putting off her international travels.

Lindy quickly found an apartment and a job in an entertainment firm. She was poised and elegant, with an olive complexion, green eyes framed by dark eyebrows, and long lashes. She was self-confident and gracious. Her politeness and good manners were authentic; she readily put people at ease.

MARK LEFT Durban in 1984, when he and his family moved to Houston. Mark attended the University of Houston, and after graduation he decided on a career in commercial real estate. Missing the ocean, he moved to Los Angeles, where real estate work was plenty and profitable. Although rent-controlled apartments in Santa Monica were hard to come by, he snatched one that was attractive and underpriced, just four blocks from where Lindy would eventually live.

Mark was tall, good-looking, athletic, and dynamic—all seemingly prerequisites for a commercial real estate agent in Los Angeles. A formidable tennis player, Mark also possessed another attractive, intangible quality: charisma. He dated frequently, with the same passion he brought to tennis, but he had no thoughts of settling down.

In 1994, nine months after Lindy arrived in California, she got a call from Mark's cousin Lisa who had once dated Lindy's brother. Lisa wanted to introduce Lindy to Mark, and she invited the two for dinner one evening.

"Mark," Lisa said, "this is Lindy. She's also from Durban."

"Nice to meet you." He shook her hand firmly.

"It's a pleasure to meet you," she replied, with a genuine smile.

"How long have you been here?" he asked.

As they began to talk about their lives, they soon discovered what an incredible feat it was that they had never met before. They were from same part of Durban, and even had some of the same teachers in school.

Every so often during dinner Lindy stole a glance at Mark. She couldn't help it—he was so striking. Mark was very animated when he spoke, exuding charm and wit, his long arms reaching across the table, his presence large and exciting. Lindy was immediately taken with him. She had never met anyone so appealing.

"I know what it's like to be new here," Mark said earnestly. "I'd be happy to show you around."

"I would love that," she replied with her usual calmness. To herself she thought, How sweet of him!

Lindy was smitten from the first. If he had taken her in his arms and professed his undying love right then, she would have experienced her own piece of heaven. But Mark treated her only as a friend. With characteristic grace, Lindy accepted his friendship and soon dismissed all thoughts of anything more.

Mark showed Lindy around L.A. as promised, and they soon became friends, talking on the phone once a week, then several times a week, and then almost all the time. As the months went by, they developed a solid, caring relationship, and they began to consider each other best friends. They shared everything and talked openly and intimately. Their day usually ended on the phone with each other, reviewing everything that had happened.

"I've been seeing Jennifer and I like her," Mark confided to Lindy one evening on the phone, "but I don't know if I like her enough to go traveling with her."

"Does she want to go away with you?" Lindy asked.

"She's already made reservations."

"I see," Lindy said. She sighed inaudibly, then gave him her take on the matter. "I don't think you should go away with her if you're not that interested. She'll only get hurt."

"You're right. I don't want to mislead her."

Mark was not an intentional heartbreaker. Women generally flocked to him, even those who were beautiful and desirable (the ones usually on the receiving end of the chase). He dated often, adored women, and thought with childlike innocence that all men were in similar straits. When he got caught in one predicament or another, Lindy was always there with sensible advice to help.

Lindy was also there when Mark dated a girl he really wanted to impress.

He would call Lindy at her office and plead, "Lindy, you have to get me a reservation at the Buffalo Club. Thursday would be great."

"I'll see what I can arrange," Lindy would offer—and always come through. The Buffalo Club was a private club frequented by people in entertainment, and through her PR firm Lindy could make reservations there.

"Thanks a million," Mark would say. "You're the best."

Their friendship continued like this for nearly two years.

Then one evening before they went out to grab a bite to eat, Mark said attentively, "You look pretty tonight, Lindy. That color suits you."

"Thank you," Lindy said, surprised. He had never commented on her appearance before. A few days later he threw her another compliment, and in other little ways began to treat her differently—with a certain tenderness. This is not like Mark, I wonder what he's up to, Lindy thought to herself, but she was too practical to make much of it.

Soon after, Mark took a short vacation to New York, where he met a woman from Peru. Dark, lithe, and stunning, she was a graduate student at New York University; after finishing her program, she was returning home to Peru. She asked Mark to visit her there, saying they could explore the Inca Trail together.

Mark thought he would like nothing better, so as soon as he got back to L.A., he booked a flight to South America.

Over dinner, Mark told Lindy all about his trip to New York. He mentioned the graduate student and the trip they'd planned.

"How exciting," Lindy said, genuinely happy for him. "To go to Peru. Hiking along the ruins. That's perfect for you, Mark."

For the first time, Mark felt funny about talking to Lindy about another woman, and he wished he hadn't said anything.

As his Peru trip neared, Mark entertained second thoughts. Three weeks before his flight, Mark and Lindy went to dinner in Marina Del Rey. They sat outside on the patio near an open fire.

"I don't think I can go to Peru," he told Lindy.

"Really? But it sounds so fantastic," Lindy said.

"It's not going to work," Mark said.

"Why not?" Lindy asked, her green eyes sparkling in the firelight.

Mark paused. As he looked intently at Lindy, he realized that in his thirty years of charmed, carefree life, he had, for the first time, stumbled upon a rare truth.

"Lindy," he said softly. "I don't want to wake up when I'm sixty years old and feel like I missed out on the best thing that ever happened to me. You're the best thing that has ever happened to me. I don't want to be away from you."

Lindy had just put a forkful of food in her mouth, and as Mark finished speaking, she began to choke. She coughed harder, turning red; Mark offered her some water. When she didn't stop coughing, he stood up to help her. She put one hand on her chest and held up the other.

"I'm all right," she managed to say. "A noodle got caught."

Finally she recovered—and her expression revealed everything: She was deliriously happy.

"Let's go away together!" Mark said suddenly. "To San Francisco!"

"Mark . . ." Lindy smiled and shook her head, marveling. It was a most unexpected turn of events.

"I'd love to, Mark."

After that night, their deep and caring friendship took a romantic turn. It turned out to be a smoother and more natural transition than either of them would have imagined. They were engaged after a year and half, and they married in December 1997.

About the Author

Author photo by Daryl Temkin

MIRIAM SOKOL is a writer who has been happily married for six years. She lives with her husband and four children in Los Angeles.

Do you have a special *How We Met* story? We would love to hear about how you met your significant other.

Please send your story to:

Miriam Sokol
c/o Prima Publishing
P.O. Box 1260BK
Rocklin, CA 95677

Or submit your story to Prima's Web site at:

HYPERLINK http://www.primalife.com/hwm

PLEASE NOTE

Prima may want to publish your story and your name in a future version of this book. By submitting a story, you agree that Prima shall own all rights to the story, including the right to publish the story and use your name in a future version of this book. Prima does not pay any compensation for the use of stories submitted. Stories should not be submitted by any person under the age of 18 and should not contain any obscene or graphic or explicit sexual material or any other illegal material of any kind.